CONJURORS: POEMS

Julian Orde (1917–74) was a granddaughter of the
4th Duke of Wellington, raised in London and
Paris, and presented at court as a debutante. She
rebelled. She achieved distinction and professional
success as a poet, a writer of short stories, an actor,
a playwright, a screenwriter and a copywriter. She
published around twenty poems in the forties, but
no more in her lifetime. Greville Press published
a pamphlet edition of her classic long poem,
Conjurors, in 1988.

James Keery lives in Culcheth with his wife Julie
and teaches English in Wigan. He has published
a collection of poems, *That Stranger, The Blues*, and
edited Carcanet's *Apocalypse*, an anthology of mid-
century visionary modernist poetry, as well as the
Collected Poems of the Scottish poet Burns Singer.

Julian Orde

edited by James Keery

Conjurors

Poems

CARCANET CLASSICS

First published in Great Britain in 2024 by
Carcanet
Alliance House, 30 Cross Street
Manchester, M 2 7 A Q
www.carcanet.co.uk

A CIP catalogue record for this book is
available from the British Library.

ISBN 978 1 80017 455 9

Book design by Andrew Latimer, Carcanet
Typesetting by LiteBook Prepress Services

The publisher acknowledges financial
assistance from Arts Council England.

CONTENTS

Introduction 9

POEMS

Postcard 19
The Surprised 19
'I would have noise that splits the head...' 20
'Treading the daisies down...' 20
'Crying neuralgia, met him in the winter...' 21
New Born 21
'Trumpets of heat...' 22
'One is white...' 22
The Use of Moths 23
Superstition 24
Winter 24
Woman Left 24
The Way of Travelling 25
'A darker faith discovers lovers' wild...' 25
The Morning Riders 26
A Petunia 27
'Drunk or alive in his arch of grief...' 27
Eve 28
Highgate Afternoon 29
Poem 31
Love 31
Mad Child 32
Their Love 32
The Awaiting Adventure 33
The Garden is Alight! 34
An Experience on Tuesday 34
Dear Dylan 36

The Upward Rain 36
The Electric Ties 36
The Way of Running 37
On Looking Out 38
Even in Such a Street 39
Makers of Wars and Poems 39
The Pool 40
Frog 41
All Night Awake 42
Eyes Alone 43
The Account 44
My Daughter to Warn Her 44
Spring Tide 45
'The hesitant pawing of the foot...' 45
The Flying Child 46
Escape in Running 48
'Without having known you...' 48
The Lonely Company 49
Fond Rebuke for a Grudged Gift 50
The Lovers 51
The Changing Wind 52
On the Boat 53
Spain-and-Juniper 53
'You were not here, you were never here...' 54
Good Friday 1947 54
The Sculptured Women of Henry Moore 55
The Six Julys of 1947 56
The Kind Sofa 57
Justice 57
Two Dogs Old 58
Time Off 59
In the Holidays 59
The Thread 60
The Only Thing to Do 61

Conjurors   62
Nijinsky   69
Roethke   70
A Man in the Garden   71
Seminar at Brussels, January 1963   72
February   73
Death in Lyndale Avenue   73
'So long ago I'd read the book...'   75
'I had known him babies ago...'   75
'Now I can love you again...'   76
'How can I use this love you do not know of?'   77
Lightness   77
'Three nuns walked in Regents Park...'   78
To a Sick Friend   78
Uninteresting Sonnet   79
Cinema   80
The Altruist   80
Two Elements   81
Mendel's Garden   82

LETTERS

Julian Orde to David Wright, 8 July 1944   85
Julian Orde to David Wright, 15 July 1944   88
Julian Orde to David Wright, 15 December 1968   93

'All in the One Number, You Me and J':
    The Poetry of Julian Orde   99

INTRODUCTION

Amongst the finest poets of the forties, Julian Orde (1914–74) was almost unknown during her lifetime and has gone under the radar for another fifty years since her death. By the end of the forties, she had published around a dozen poems, appeared in *The Listener*, and contributed to two prestigious American collections, James Laughlin's annual *New Directions* (No. 10, 1948) and Kenneth Rexroth's classic anthology of neo-romanticism, *The New British Poets* (1949). Yet she never published another poem. Only a single one carries a date in the fifties, and it may well be that she wrote very little poetry during the decade, before beginning again to write and submit poems in the sixties. Out of the blue, in 1968, Robin Skelton selected 'The Changing Wind' for the Penguin anthology, *Poetry of the Forties*, and in 1969 an American poet, Ian Young, took the first line from another forties poem, 'The Use of Moths', for an epigraph to one of his own, but it was only after her death that she began to attract more than occasional interest. 'Conjurors', appeared in *Poetry Nation* in 1976; David Wright edited a selection of fifteen poems for *PN Review* in 1978; and ten years later, in 1988, Greville Press published her only independent work, *Conjurors*, a pamphlet edition of her wonderful long poem.

'Conjurors' is undated, but I would agree with David Wright in assigning it to the late forties. In the 'Note' which accompanied her set in *PN Review*, he rises to the occasion:

> 'Conjurors' is not only Julian Orde's masterpiece, it is a masterpiece. If the poem was put away to lie unregarded in a drawer, that must be because she must have known it was not of a kind to catch any of the various poetic bandwagons that trundled by

after 1950. The poem obeys an elaborate metric, a complex stanza-form and rhyme-scheme, not artificial or arbitrary but perfectly fitted to its matter, sustained over two hundred lines. W.S. Graham was a close friend; it may be that the discipline and technical control deployed in the poem owes something to him, though the voice, cadence, and diction are entirely her own. The language is plain without being drab (one of the rewards of passing through the neo-romantic fire). The poem is about the metamorphosis of caterpillars. A meticulous record of the process, from grub to chrysalis to imago. No very promising subject; yet the poem succeeds. It is even exciting. Description, yet more than description; the observation is detailed, but attention is held, for the poem is not static: it has a narrative pull that tugs the reader from one stanza to the next. Also it has that mysterious effect, a quality of poetry, of saying more than appears; what's more, without having to erect a scaffolding of obtrusive symbolism ... The poet's eye sees, and makes the reader's see with equal precision; yet the metamorphosis the poem celebrates and achieves is more than that of caterpillar into butterfly.

'Such truth as makes continual surprise', a line from 'Postcard', the first poem collected here, is an apt account of Julian Orde's poetry, the true speech of dream and vision. One who 'Grew never used to life or ceased surprise' ('The Account'), finding 'Always a new incredible minute to crown / Twenty six years of surprise' ('The Electric Ties'), she encapsulated her enchantment with the dailiness of things in 'The Way of Running', with recourse yet again to one of her favourite words: 'I ran with a love for running and no more / Across the vast and genius surprise / Of morning'. And surprise can turn dark side out, as in another early poem, 'The Surprised':

> I have ridden streets of apricot but found my heart
> Most often in the enemy cellars of a fear.
> And have seen most truly staring into nightmare dark,
> While in a full cry of gladness missed my way.

Julian Orde was one of the stand-out contributors to the Carcanet anthology of the mid-century, *Apocalypse* (2020). One poem, 'The Awaiting Adventure', was selected for reading during the Zoom launch by Simon Armitage, who described the poet he had just discovered as 'something of a mystery all round'. Her distinctive voice was warmly appreciated by William Empson, who knew the poet but had never read her poetry: 'I was surprised to find it so good ... Wonder at nature, wonder at all experience, is her note, and she gets a great deal of variety into it; also she has a beautiful ear, and a supply of unforced humour'. It is high time she took her place alongside her close friends, W.S. Graham and David Wright, as, on one occasion, she already had, in *Poetry Quarterly* in 1945, to Graham's delight: 'all in the one number, you me and J'.

A niece of two Dukes of Wellington, Julian Orde was raised in London and Paris, and presented at court as a debutante. Estranged from her family from the early forties, she was living in poverty with a daughter from a brief affair with a refugee Polish pilot. Her Highgate flat became a rendezvous for the poets and painters of Soho when this legendary artistic scene was at its most vibrant. 'A Jill of all trades', according to Wright, she mastered all of them, achieving distinction and professional success as a poet, a writer of short stories, an actor, a playwright, a screenwriter and a copywriter. In later life, she took up photography, winning a *Sunday Times* award. And 'last of all', as Wright recalls, 'filled her house with brilliant flower-canvases, till one hardly knew where the sitting-room ended and the long garden behind the bay-windows began'. It is as a poet, however, that she demands attention. Her first collection, this overdue book presents more than sixty poems, of which only around twenty have ever been published. Julian Orde's lyrical surrealism creates a space of its own and will appeal to many readers.

Note on the Text

When I was first invited to edit a collection by Julian Orde, it would have been a light task and a slim volume – so slim there would scarcely have been room for her name on the spine. Her complete poetical works consisted of twenty lyrics and one long poem, 'Conjurors'. The title-poem had been published in *Poetry Nation* in 1976, then fifteen lyrics were printed in *PN Review* in 1978. Half of these and a handful of others had appeared in poetry magazines during the forties, and apart from a couple of short stories, that was it. There was no sign of the 'parcel' from her daughter Emily Abercrombie, from which David Wright had made his *PNR* selection. Then, in the course of editing Wright's letters, V. Beatson, his step-daughter, rediscovered not one but two large packets, the first containing just under a hundred poems and the second another fifty, together with letters and sketches, and later correspondence between Wright, Emily Abercrombie, William Empson, C.H. Sisson and Michael Schmidt.

Conjurors features 80 of Orde's 150 extant poems (a few more have recently come to light, mainly prize-winning light verse from *Time & Tide* and *The New Statesman*). I have included all of her published poems, together with all but six of the long list of 45 made by David Wright when editing the *PNR* feature. He included a number of untitled drafts, and I have added several more. Few even of her slightest, least finished pieces lack a memorable image or cadence.

Ten poems carry dates; the rest are undated. I have used any available evidence, including biographical details or datable occasions. Orde's successive addresses are more or less datable, but often appear on submissions to magazines, perhaps years after any given poem was written. Emily Abercrombie initially typed up 67 numbered poems, 'one block of 28 poems under Mum's original index – then another block starting from 29–67'. Not even the 28 poems in 'Mum's Original Index' (lost, but most identifiable from numbered copies) are in exact chronological order. Consecutively numbered poems, even poems stapled together, may date from different years, though all appear to be from the forties, and No. 28, 'The Six Julys of 1947', may well be the latest. The dates given in the text appear on a typescript or manuscript of a poem; dates of publication are also recorded, since, like addresses, these supply a *terminus ad quem*, though in some cases the conjectural date of the poem itself is a year or more earlier. The key word here is 'conjectural'.

'Conjurors' is particularly hard to date, as Wright notes: 'I don't know when it got written; my guess would be before her marriage in 1950 to Ralph Abercrombie, when Julian was living alone either at Highgate or Muswell Hill. Yet the mature style points to a later date'. On the other hand, its interrelationship with 'The Flying Child', published in *Poetry Quarterly* in the summer of 1947, would tend to support Wright's own 'guess', a date in the late forties.

Not a single poem is definitely assignable to the years 1951–61. From 1950 until 1955, and perhaps for the rest of the decade, Orde was living with her husband at 4, The Park, Highgate, an address which appears only on a single poem, 'Nijinsky', an elegy for the ballet dancer who died on 8 April 1950. Drafts of an elegy for Robert Colquhoun may be assumed to date from shortly after his death on 20 September 1962. By 1963, Orde had moved to 38 Lyndale Avenue, in Child's Hill, an address which appears on several poems, with more in a similar typeface. In between, one poem, 'Roethke', might be linked with the poet's breakthrough British collection, *Words for the Wind*, in 1957; and it is quite possible that a number of poems, conjecturally dated earlier or later, may date from the fifties, but it seems safe to conclude that this was a fallow period.

I include three of a dozen letters to David Wright, preserved with the poems. The two written during the 'P Bomb' or doodlebug summer of 1944 are of profound historical as well as personal interest. The 1968 letter presents more facets of a single life than most biographies.

POEMS

POSTCARD

Old friend, what time is it in your brave life?
How are the towns you planted in the spring?
Build you a hill today? What makes your wife?
Is she a song, a wall of sound for your weight,
Like the hard top of the sea or the leaning wind?
Who is your summer's child? Gods could not bear
More lovely child than you woke up last year.
I smile to know you warm the walking earth
There, to my left, changing some view, some green
West view I love but only have not seen.
Write me a letter round with your looking eyes,
Such truth as makes continual surprise!
Tell me your time, do not leave out your heart.
Salute from me, old friend, all you create.

THE SURPRISED

I have ridden streets of apricot but found my heart
Most often in the enemy cellars of a fear.
And have seen most truly staring into nightmare dark,
While in a full cry of gladness missed my way.
I followed the lovely, rushing birds and found a net.
And when I fled a monster I fled my brother.
And trembling in my hands I saw the moon turn over.
And I shall never learn because the rule escapes me,
And I shall never regret because the faith is in me,
But I will ride my good, high horse until he throws me.

'I WOULD HAVE NOISE THAT SPLITS THE HEAD...'

I would have noise that splits the head in twain,
And light that blinds, and darkness thick and black,
And smells that reel the senses, like a train
Of gaudy sweet-meats. And all along the track,
Colour, most garish. And large drops of rain
Like dark pearls, and in the sky, a crack
As of a chariot-race, and wine-red stain
And speed! Like ice, nor ever turning back!

And I would have joy that lifts the feet like wind,
And sorrow, grey as twilight's veil, and long
As Death's own river. And love, no mind
As ever thought on; oh love, so strong,
That to all noise, am deaf, all colour, blind,
All senses stone where love does not belong.

'TREADING THE DAISIES DOWN...'

Treading the daisies down with steps of silver
The ghost came swaying sideways to the house
Followed by many who could never rouse
Dogs from their sleep or butler with a salver
Or wake a moth. These, like the shadowy elver
Who slips away half round all seas, to cows
In the clover by the country pond and owes
Nothing but wonder – These followed the miller.

Into the house were sucked the flickering twelve
White shadows, till the house was a praying nation
Calling for cease of war when the extreme
Childhood of their fear begins to delve

Through the last webs of the grownup ration
And they cry to wake and know it's not a dream.

'CRYING NEURALGIA, MET HIM IN THE WINTER...'

Crying neuralgia, met him in the winter
Blood heat, he said, in his gum like a drum
I too had a heart without a home
To the company unlikely would saunter
In the dark room, & the bright bottles, spent a
While looking for love, then saw him.
So I wasn't after all out on a limb.
Near Camden Town things went with a canter

Down came such a rook of a cloud
Off my balance and no alert,
I will say aloud I am not proud
Of the way my lover and I were hurt
Sometimes I go as dead as a shroud.
But he blows me back, so loving is his heart.

NEW BORN

This cast-off animal from cradling waters
That has no tongue not carried from the spheres,
Nor wisdom but the summer seedlings' vows,
In perfect splendour waits upon the world.
The prism injects knowledge to filmed eyes,
The curious rolling air sips the new skin.
The arrangement to live is now being tried.
Silence comes from the trees and every house.

Tomorrow's composition must regroup for welcome,
Must yield, the old stigmata of the sky;
Sorrow away, and passengers for Christmas
Shall light a candle to this vaulted heart,
Staying, because such terrible purity
Lies somewhere among the ordinary dusts.

'TRUMPETS OF HEAT...'

Trumpets of heat blared London in the sun.
Grey footed I, at noon, lame with a child,
Saw a dim mirrored room, a couch of green,
Cool, pale, still in a sinking pool,
A forever dipping, dripping silence of silk,
Held in a ball of time, for on and on.
I would be spreading soft on the green bed
With the sore streets remembered in my limbs
And the trumpets still rocking my poor head.
I'd lie there, drifting away from all memory
Into the infinite caverns of the mirrors,
Aware of my sleep, thanksgiving for my death.

Knowing that I shall never know this peace,
I build a room – and break it with a breath.

'ONE IS WHITE...'

One is white in a murmuring hospital evening,
Living from each slow blown bubble of breath,
With Christmas swaying the candles and over the earth,
Christmas in a pain of innocence and children,
To honour the good with our own black, bare hands.

She is a mountain away, iron in her bed
With a war in her throat, and shouting from her eyes,
White in the dry, unbreathing hospital air,
While Christmas touches with faint carols her world
Of one, of an only truth; may she not die.

THE USE OF MOTHS

Moths were made for the pleasure of candles.
In her salty grave the fish-wife turned and said:
'Moths were made for the pleasure of candles,
But these grey fish are my muscular last bed'.

The cod were naked as any woman
Under an icicle tree the gardeners adored.
'Beautiful children!' mourned the woman,
'My heart-warm daughter gave joy to a frozen sword.

I miss the bees in this weight of water,
Each bee's a day I thought when I was a kid,
Each day was a palace I built, but later
I knew the roof was the echoing bone of my head.

Moths were made for the pleasure of candles,
That was my faith', the fish woman, groaning, said,
'But the sea has no pity for dry, bright candles,
So I sway with the cod in the night of my last bed'.

Poetry Quarterly, Spring 1946

SUPERSTITION

Carry her to market on a crimson shutter,
Black boys bury her, shiver her with salt!
She split the moon with a darning needle,
She pulled dead Jeremy from the vault.
> Down from the houses shall treadle her a canopy –
> Fish nets swinging in a wet sea wind;

Goodbye, witch-woman, fine and rosy
Your heels go trotting on the window blind.
I think I saw her fingering parsley.
Once I heard her plotting with a spider.
> Carry her to market on a crimson shutter,
> And let me watch from the castle wall.

Voices, No. 3, 1944

WINTER

Across the Highgate hills night of the year
Sweeps away summer lives and mine has gone,
Outridden by the hardy and the young
In their red hoods bright in the bitter day.

WOMAN LEFT

I am more hundred times alone
Because my love is gravely gone.
The quickest dash of blood or flame
Is not so quick as brings him home.
No flame, no blood is there that warms
The wastes between these world-wide arms.

THE WAY OF TRAVELLING

Under my thoughts, the green man's stammered journey
Always unended, calls to my smile again;
Now he has springs, sweet flowering in his bonnet;
Now struts, now sidles, chaffering to the rain.

Now claps the dust, quick-jaunty from his shoulders,
Now stops, dumbfoundered, learning a sparrow's song,
Now runs till winded to pay back the minute,
Now belches, yawns and jeers himself along.

Under my thoughts the old road stretches thinly,
The green man dancing on it to the sky;
Minds not the none to praise his daring laughter,
Or gape from hidden couch to watch him cry.

Because he capers in my dreadful pauses,
His ordinary braveness calls my own:
Three thousand million men are on a journey,
And each, maybe, is travelling alone.

May 1944

'A DARKER FAITH DISCOVERS LOVERS' WILD...'

A darker faith discovers lovers' wild
Wishing and welcoming tumult of embrace
Than makes the sea push
Or sails an oceaned moon to space
Cast up by mineral battle round a world
When iron lovers wrestled for a wish.

A lonelier faith by witches' sons goes crying
Deep to the always wooden always deaf
Son of another she,
Farming son of the burying earth.
There where he grinds his human lover, lying
Like a star above her he is crying unknowing to be
His unanswering, happier brother, blade of green corn
Paired on the stem of his love all his summers long.

THE MORNING RIDERS

Yes, where the chariots are racing out
Lives the beginning and users of the morning.
Grasp in a cherishing palm, users of grace!
The hill is locked to the blind heel, the turning
Of water splits the passion in a face.
Even the riders launched under a poor sky
Must whisper-down their difference and gentle
Their step and sight, so that the crowned may people
Their hill-tops with brave lovers and good ones.
The honoured free must priestly hold their freedom.

The unoceaned beaches where the unloved lie
Stare on, as strings of time are pegged down mutely.
No choruses proudly render psalms to holiday
For the pleasant gift of living a green calendar.
The unreligious know not when they die.
Even the liars got in a rare bed
Unmake their grandeur with a stale surprise;
Through them the roar of heaven is limited,
And midgets scatter down the unnoticed valleys,
Beading their prayers because their gods are dead.

The stallioned and throned are ready with wide wise open eyes
To bear the hurtling appetites and scapegoat wealth of worlds.

May 1944

A PETUNIA

According to the purple petunia it is close on nine.
She is about to die and weakly drapes our summertime in folds.
At noon she had balanced truly for two hours in the sun,
After a morning of devotedly and delicately becoming unfurled.
For three grass months she had followed her plans,
Examining each hissing inch of earth, drawing the wild
Tempers from every climate that swerved near, deciding
Which were her elements for beauty out of the whole world.
At noon she had balanced truly for two hours in the sun,
Completely and essentially a petunia. It was perfectly done.

'DRUNK OR ALIVE IN HIS ARCH OF GRIEF...'

Drunk or alive in his arch of grief
I loved this melancholy man
Who sailed his words like a flock of boats
And wrecked them on his tongue
Who tamed an elephant in secret
And let it trample him down,
Because he could not love himself
Or find his innocence again.
Starveling as the moon was I
He could not change my money,
He could not take a tear from me
Or anyone, he was so lonely,

But gold doubloons he threw about
And did not watch who picked them up.
And he built new faces for his friends
Out of their old stories,
And he built a bookcase out of a bottle
And gave it to a library.
Drunk or alive in his house of grief
I loved this melancholy man
Who locked the door where we go in
Then lost the key and wept and ran
And recognised he was alone.

EVE

Sunblinded
            From my unkind
Birth, remembering
            The garden throwing
Itself on me,
            The windy
Lung's scream
            When the air jumped in,
The long shadow
            Of Adam, so:
Plurality.
            Quickest took me:
The garden galloping
            All its green
Down through my
            Empty eyes.
My eardrums finally
            Were hardened by
Continual
            Creak of a mill.

'Admit my weight,'
      Said the planet,
On every branch
      Of my flesh
It rose and hung;
      My body sharing,
Would not be rid.
      I had started
My double journey:
      Earth and history.
Had never stepped
      Light as a child,
Had never known
      Watery womb,
Or turned over
      Inside a mother.
A poor thing,
      My derivation,
A thin bone
      Stood alone.
Still am I seeking
      Compensation.

HIGHGATE AFTERNOON

I love. The musical houses are slanting into streets.
My wide window draws in a population of cities
And beating birds, and the first egg-pecking of assembled orchestras.

Row upon row of green trees quietly grow.

The crescent hemisphere of spires are tuning up their strings
Because the town moves now more fast in a heart's direction,
And I am flinging my old coat higher than I can reach.

The dear musician, all a world to westward, lives now.

O I have a planetarium of unsung stars for him!
And my house is infinite and my window wide and my arms wide,
Shoaled with the straying and creeping-in as they stretch for him.

(I can see the round of sorrow, for all spins in this town.)

I can hear the roar of loving gathering sound along the evening,
Cast through the singing wires, echoed in stone hallways, chimed
From a park set swinging on three chains, buzzing through fire,
Tightened to the light and death of one spark, loosed out in a
river,
Carried in water away beyond the daggered rim of the city.

My round eye's memory sees more than it can measure now.

2

Because one parachuting seed, soft rocking on a breath
Might in Marazion grow a green city, lift Germoe
From its cobblestones or drum Pengersick Lane to Wheelhouse
To find his easy heart and bind with green his caravan,
I will blow and I will blow my seeds to Marazion and Germoe.

A soft population of swaying seeds are being sent to westward.

The long salt octaves are his sleep song there,
To roll his pillow in the home-sick miles of a sea's sigh.
How far that makes him seem ... how almost reaching goodbye ...

Wave upon wave upon wave of green seas slumber him brave.

I love. Addressing all ministers of wandering spires and wits:
This Thursday cottaged the first quick survey of adventure;
I have not done, the listening is all, and this:

That we are happy as our lovers see us, and such we are.

POEM

      The morning weaves
A piece of bone
      To a branch of fingers,
But the rain
      Blurs the sea-shift
Twists the cone,
      And now this hand
Is bone again.

LOVE

Thrust your winters and summers through me
Drawn by the surge of my love and spring,
Lay your climate and country on me,
We are a world and round is this meeting.
Fill my womb with the jump of your joy,
I would drown in the waves of your coxcomb sea.

I yield my secret childhood to you,
The house where I grew and the dream I made,
Nothing I keep in this surrender,
It is your splendour that builds my pride.
All that I ever was, all that I am,
Encloses my lover, the sum of my wonder.

MAD CHILD

His mind is a bud
Forever folded;
His thoughts are sealed
In his lolling head.
Though he listen so soft
No whisper breaks
The trembling silence
Of his life.
The pictured facets
Of sensation
Must stay his secret,
For he treads
The deadly parallel.
Till his lonely dying
He'll not discover
What is our language
Nor shall we find his.

THEIR LOVE

Dark as the heart as the green black shadow where the crystals ride
Strung on the thin grey threads of a web spun for no reason,
Dark as the forest where the rotted and springing are plaited in silence,
Was the beginnings of this earth-thick heaviness of love,
Brick-dusty, noon dust, heave of the heave of their love,
(Born in the dark of the mind in the worm and the curl of the brain,)
Honey warm now, flame of the molten flame,
From the central movement of Earth, from the liquid rock!
And if it ended, not in the blown brown leaves,
Not in the dancer's spangles, tongues or the pavement's edge
Or the crest of a lesser beading seething bubbles sliding on a string –
But only the pillars may break, the roof of reason crumble,

As Samson rocks the columns in his numb, red hands,
Till the white sky bursting upward leaves him exposed in his proudness
In his triumph in his puissance in his oneness
In his only goodly godly lonely manly final *deadness*!

THE AWAITING ADVENTURE

Dear stranger, the mule is loaded, let us start.
A tune of trees is written across the hill,
And the sky is high, today, and nothing is still,
But I feel banners thudding against a wind,
A cave of wings rushing over the ground,
And the leaping day calling me into love.

The expert from the city tunes the trees
In far snowfields of sleep we may not cross;
The revolving lighthouse is adrift and lost –
But oh! I am awake and running down
The yellow slopes of my tomorrow's hopes!

There is about us more than a man's mind,
More than a ship's huge voyaging and end
Or the whole brass music of a gallant day.
The jet of life has sprung its ecstasy:
I am in love with greater than I am,
And share the way of stone and star and lamb,
And even the central, liquid rock moves in me.

Always, stranger, let us be setting out,
With home not left but in ourselves always.
The eager fabulist of holy orders
Will log our journey for us in the night,
And – if we let him – ride ahead and praise.

The hierarchy of mountains does not speak,
But the cold flowers, with a different life,

And in a different time, create and die,
Familiar with the deathless walls of ice;
Not seeing their fathers' shape against the sky.

Stranger, met at last, this great beginning
Shall swing us through all times and all planes;
Though we but walk, are little, and have names,
Our history is in us and we in history.

April 1945

THE GARDEN IS ALIGHT!

Oh look, and look, the garden is alight!
Nothing resists or withers in the fire,
Sap sings, all wrapped in flame;
Nasturtiums roar and sparkle as they burn,
For every leaping flower was once the leaping sun!

Frogs, lions and spindle-stalking crane
Come glimmering through the garden's wedding pyre;
Under the blue and bending sky
Blown poppies offer ripples of desire
And golden beetles praise the petals of the sun!

AN EXPERIENCE ON TUESDAY

  Listen you others:
I was lit by the flint and steel of my love on Tuesday,
  Sparked into love,
Giant-strode over the streets and mastered the wheelways,
  Could see in a round,
Yes, and time, opening and shutting its pleats like a fan,

Waited for me.
The tickertape brains were unwinding in rolls at my feet,
　　　I laughed and cried
With the breast of the crowd as it pressed out its laughter or tears.
　　　I got entangled
In a picture, with fruit, I remembered from peppermint times,
　　　– A pear in a fire –
Once again I was lost in the pulses of colour, confused
　　　In the land of a pear
In the porphyry hall of a house where I marbled the hours.
　　　So human a love
I could hear even India, with a mosquito hum
　　　In hollow Chelsea,
And a suddenly thick, hot shiver from Africa
　　　Stopped my breath
In a flat gasp, corked on the side of a jungle leaf.
　　　My mother and father
Grew small, to children, to lizards, fish and away.
　　　I in my grave
Enormously spread till my final and separate cells
　　　Covered the earth.
Tuesday boiled up, left its essence the evening
　　　Spilling over me,
Which I drank in the name of my splendid and cauldron thirst.
　　　Such a draught!
Taste of wet trees and fish-river and roof warm slates.
　　　I was tired by night;
The wheels I had mastered were turning and rolling me over,
　　　A house stood up
And I watched it come crashing and crushing me, lolling my head.
　　　My steel flint love
That had sparked me alight was worn out and my love was dead.
　　　Wednesday – and dead.

'V.E. Day', 8 May 1945

DEAR DYLAN

Dear Dylan oh why did you
Not ring me up?
I fear the Young Dog
Has sold me a pup.

We will meet once a year when
The Wheatsheaf is dry
And you'll tell me a story
And once more I'll buy.

My arches are fallen
My morals laid low
Forsaken by Dylan
– yours faithfully – JO

THE UPWARD RAIN

Dropped, let fall with a sigh, the clouds have released rain;
The brown earth hisses and swarms up the silver branches,
Green climbs to the sky till the clouds are swelling with flowers.
Splashed come the fruit and the bees and the waves of the tree;
Flashing wet metal, there is sudden arrival of dragonflies,
Held in the air by their rigid and quivering wings like church windows.
Such a meeting of water and lovers of water I see!
Such communion of flower and cloud and the waves of the tree!

New Road No. 4, 1946

THE ELECTRIC TIES

Without doubt, whirring in dusty sun,
In a dry to the tongue uncoloured August town

Went six electric ties.
How odd from the bus stop staring down,
Their regular flicker made satin as busy as fins
Or as bright flickering eyes.
No end no end to broken lines,
Always a new incredible minute to crown
Twenty six years of surprise.

20 July 1945 (aged 27)

THE WAY OF RUNNING

A furious pillar I ran from the folded lake
Dumb with no eyes or mouth in the humped night
In the turning-away, the ungenerous, beggaring dark.
Looked for you under umbrellas of marrow flowers,
In a long tree hollowing round a grim
Grave grinning man who bit my questioning hands.
Screamed through a hedge of pins red with prayers
And swooned dead down upon an unnoticing town
Of grass people cold in their green houses.
A wood's one bird slipped out a curved note
Lost as a lunatic sad in his sky's mind.
The country heavy night pressed soft as toads.
So passed that autumn dying out of doors,
Starred in a cross against the meadow's side.

Remembering – chameleon in my sleep –
Those high-stalked days among the walking grass,
That field-wide breast that took me like a god.
And there was a tree that was my father, yes,
Before youth – was it? – in the peppermint air
Where every new experimenting world
Rushed like a flock of boats across the lake.
There with bats' wings made horses, caught and drew

All leathern crescents to my gentle hands
Launching their shapes among the mild grass winds
Until, myself in everywhere, I flew.
I would return again to find the tree
That was my father, yes, and the white sound
The wide white sound in my head, rocking me.

The mushroom morning and a day for kites
Struck me awake amid the brilliant cows
Moving to meet the colours of sunrise.
I ran with a love for running and no more
Across the vast and genius surprise
Of morning. The grass was hung with cuckoo-spit
And the string man dangled, waiting in my mind.
But while I ran I only could adore
Running, because it is no use trying to find
A lover in a marrow flower, a father
Stalking for always the earth like a proud tree.
It is no use going back at all for we
Are wiser in this running minute than ever
Before we were or are ever likely to be.

14 September 1945

ON LOOKING OUT

A mushroom morning and a day for kites,
And the rickshaw boys bickering in China,
And myself in the middle of the middle ring,
(But everyone else thinks they are);
And a skyscape just arrived, with quite
Its best and unrepeatable design, a
Water-land built solid out of nothing,
And beautiful as my imagined China.

Poetry Quarterly, Summer 1947

EVEN IN SUCH A STREET

My daughter's sleep spreads wide as a far prairie.
They are not aware of it in Hiroshima or Khartoum,
How it pours from the child's orange-box room.

Throwing itself downhill now bangs a lorry
And my house jumps. Stronger is the wireless story,
Replacing the house altogether with a village and some
Irishmen talking with words like wood carvings.
(Ships in the air! Oh this is being at home.)

This is being at home where the tides are going
Inwards and outwards, sending and bringing
What the deep heart listens for: news
Of brothers, sleep of children, the brushing near
Of the unknown lorry-driver's rope of noise.

It is all here. It is all here, even here.

MAKERS OF WARS AND POEMS

My daughter's sleep
      Spreads wide as a far prairie.
      Outside go the violent lorries
Making the house leap.
More strong her sleep
      Than the rattling of winged cages,
      Than the going of time's paces
More swift her sleep.

The poem I read
      Comes up with a burning and a roaring
      Let loose in a column of glory,

And down go house and street.
Stronger than house shall leap
  When backwards and forwards we've gone
  Finding at last we are all one
Maker of war or sleep.

THE POOL

Up came my face through coloured rings of water,
A foot trailed still the tunnel from Australia.
The sun pool met fish-flashing in their pleasure,
Pitch peacock trees loomed near with masked expression.
Hell and the hills boiled misty miles away,
A black white snapping was the nights and days
Of a world at hand turning to a different tune.

My weedy face forever floating up
Never quite broke the flat of the pool's shine.
Below, the rings evenly grew to vanish.
Knowledge of children on another side
Made wise a town of rough and shuttled hands,
Knowledge of sea foamed not a field of corn
And tickled with its salt message a child of sorrel.
Knowledge of birds excited the loving pool;
Birds and the sucking sun sparkled her bed.
Witch warlock trees knew only their black shade.

She in his eyes saw funnels to Australia,
He wound his death each night while seven cells
Storked into sons made seven eternities.
Frogs ticked on summer, paler frogs in bottles
Taught a biologist plans of a northern bear.
Atoms grew gardens. Spun of his garden hair
Grave grasses took again her long lost hands.

The fourth perpendicular, the foreign tower,
Extended flowers into invisible lands,
Reflected cubically the absence of a plover.
Five lustres sprung a man to lionhood,
Fifteen carried him down and redesigned
The atlas of his future voyagings
With a double compass set for Gemini.
Not lost the red heart of his lustihood
Nor the hopeful holy visions in his mind
But proof as the ultimate structure of a diamond.

So did the disparate worlds tick and drone,
Kingdoms in skeletons, atoms in hive and heaven.
Not beginning not ending going on going on going on
Repeated the cities, beat out the hugely hidden
Hammering rhyme of rock, rocking in space.
Up through the water swam always my green face
And the hills knew always a scatter of children down.

FROG

The speckled water rippled into minnows,
Of worms and turf smelt all the fish pale morning,
Earth pushed up its smell of worms through grass and wet,
Through sodden leaf, mushroom and winking frog.
I, on the bank, lived quick as breathing frog,
Its lungs and mine puffed out September's thin
Morning, sallow and silver, fish-filled, the sky in a river.

Wherever I go in the guilty years there still
Goes my innocence with me. Still can I live like the frog,
With its visible heartbeat ticking its love for the frog-
Made morning, both holder and giver, earth and river,
Receiver and breather, a leaf with no stem, a lover
Of shallows and shadows, of flies on the tongue, of stones,
I cannot be seven again but the frog is again by the river.

ALL NIGHT AWAKE

The growing up morning is rising round my house
     Like tall white women.
The beginning clock puts trees; birds begin.
     But I am yesterday
Wearing a lost coat, left over, merely
     Dragged on the wheels
Across into morning-time with resisting heels,
     Sick and bombarded
With the signs of arrival to stay of a day; unguarded.
     I crossed this corridor
Wanting to watch my cheated nerves; explore.
     I saw grey girls
Endlessly opening doors in silence and tears.
     Going away
In a light was the King of Fright, his crown and shadow.
     You may ask:
What tune or geometry resolved this unnatural task?
     The thin fingers
Strangling down on the bounding ball of wings?
     Or the pooled window
Gathering bundles of trees and preparing for morrow?
     What tune or geometry
Was finally lined by a lover of order, discovery?
     I can only repeat:
I felt the slow the quick of the world's and the heart's beat,
     The loud the soft
Of the snow squeak underfoot and the snow in a drift,
     The soft the sharp
That is cats, the low the high view of my toe and eye,
     The turning two ways
Of a planet, the alternately hissing and stilling of stars.
     My body divided,
Slid away from the bones with a snarl with a bag of wool,

Spun through the gate,
Went spinning an angry thread round an empty estate
And never came back.
My window has gathered the morning into its lake.
I am left hollow.
My window is putting up trees and preparing for morrow.

New Directions in Prose and Poetry No. 10, 1948

EYES ALONE

My vision suddenly springing clear of me
Enjoys an unremembered, unpassionate place
And sees bold out-of-doors without a face.
Adam of landscapes! Quick and bare of me.

Treading the wound-up world, mountains in irons
Converge below horizon's birth of water
Until is launched the first of fire and father:
The sun roars upward with a crew of lions.

Twelve wings all feathering in a town of swords
Make lights across the bridal porch and sky
And twelve white lilies steal delicately by
Swaying like women through an arch of birds.

As strange it is as Eve's defenceless waking
When the garden surged into her naked eyes
To meet no other summer green of memories.
A rib stood staring, raped headlong by a garden.

Without myself my vision draws to no end,
The soothsayer's mouth is fastened round his song,
Basket or grave have both some sort of man,
And faces shift like a bush of leaves in the wind.

THE ACCOUNT

The elephant-gear of my tremendous lust
Will finally turn into the quiet forest
The stamping godhead din me into deafness
And my all-gathering eyes collect up darkness.
The sum of each encounter and new message
Checked and forgotten will be, like pain, like rage.
The calculated weight of happiness
Balanced uneven and fallen sideways.
Sorrow all dried to a salt stain, regret
Reasoned to nothing. Then what shape of spirit
Will I have left to offer? Might I say:
'I loved without wisdom, took, and gave away,
Carried no weapon but praised much, and besides
Grew never used to life or ceased surprise?'

February 1946

MY DAUGHTER TO WARN HER

Call not sweet words to the mouth, my daughter,
Nor claim barbarian honour in the spring,
Nor wait until the lententide of slaughter,
When bones and bells do cariously ring.
You must not hear the murmurous houses sing
Below the trellised beaches of the farm,
Or lean your head under the fountain's wing
To rouse the pallid sleepers of alarm.

Lest for your wedding there be farthings sold,
Mouth not the tender buds of secret pride;
Or dance, bewildered for a puppet's gold,
Or snatch the treasure from the thrush's bride.

My mothering steps might lead to find you cold,
Starred in a cross upon the mountain side.

SPRING TIDE

The emperor arms of the beech rise strong
And muscled like rivers above my head
While the young leaves toss in a purple flood;
Green drops hang from the cedar black –
Oh send me your hare's foot heart for luck,
I feel the whirlpools of the spring.

I would be sprouting too, would grow
The green curve of a fountain's wing,
Startling and innocent, for you.
All roughening winters rinsed away,
Unfurl a brilliant heart this May,
Washed by the light waves of the spring.

'THE HESITANT PAWING OF THE FOOT...'

The hesitant pawing of the foot upon unknown edges,
The wire drawn thin and the dancer hurrying over,
Reaching where tested places, bare with habit, are ready,
Nor need for the panic sight behind the shoulder.

The eyes are listening where fists are torn on the shutter,
The heart not listening to the long tread of the blind;
Caught in a corridor of held breath, hearing
The cold dry murmur of hospitals by night.

Constructed of dust and feathers and fishes' bones,
The children's castles glittered in the park.

And out there to smell is know; not green the fields,
Not white the snow, not old the dead but dark in blood.

Only the lover can, for a moment, come down like an angel,
Folding and warming away from night and the precipice;
Then nearly, nearly is safe as the homesick womb,
And nearly is one, and near is escape in a miracle.

THE FLYING CHILD

Constructed of feathers and fishes' bones
The kicked-over castles were drifts of dust
That the children left when the whistle blew
In the Luxembourg Gardens, long ago.
And when, with a caught moth terrifying
My fingers and thumbs, I rose and flew
Out of the locked gates and the park,
In people's houses they found it tea-time;
But the convict moth opposed a midnight.

A thief in despair, my hands were stones,
And nothing so feeling as membrane moth
(Presented to pain down a thousand hairs)
Had ever cruelly crashed in the dark;
And nothing so brittle and insect eye-lashed
Had crackled and fluttered in such a den.
(No voice it had, to print in the air
A crippled copy of harm and hurt.
That was the worst, the loneliest thought.)

It began to grow. So terrified then
Was my den of hands that could not know
If they should be broken or tarnished moth
Stain on them always a dusty death,

That I came to the ground in an avenue,
And opened my thumbs, and stopped the clap
Of wings, by holding them, skin to skin.
Then in full cry I went blazing back
To the hunting place in the evening park
To give to the wind its moth and kin.

Empty the Luxembourg garden of all
But its skeleton self, with a sigh breathing
Through railing and rattling laurel leaves
And urn and wind-washed stone and tall
Triangular trees and other trees.
Where five grey castles stood before,
Round the iron-clawed seats were deeper drifts,
Arrowed with fish-bone, horned with twig,
To screech a shoe on the glass and grit,
On a button that opened a castle door.

A multiplication of pain – the moth.
I saw the generations lying
Between its wings. I peeled one off
And watched it meet and change the sky
With a hind's breast, with a life forgiven,
Black as a whistle, out of a deathbed.
And into birds they all were startled,
Till the ruffed and feathered air was shaken,
And with bird brows my head was circled.

Then the last moth fell, soft-bodied, foetal,
Flopped to the gravel; became a cat.
The garden ground crept forward with it,
It dragged the night behind its heel,
And wildest bird could not migrate from that.

Poetry Quarterly, Summer 1947

ESCAPE IN RUNNING

I ran until I left myself behind me;
I speared my thoughts onto a spire of pain and left them.
Into the cleft of road and hedge
I, with the sound of morning on my face,
Streamed past the finished things and into day.

Five little towns were humming in the valley,
The telegraph trees were warm, and lonely, throbbing;
The road was roughened with unsorted stones.

I was the hollow can for the wash of the air,
No claim nor count but I was the holder and giver;
And I was the pulse of the green-shot world and driven
With the fountains of growth to the split-wide edge of blue,
Hurling my love in a torrent of worthy shapes
And crying the names of the just for the just to hear.

Poetry Quarterly, Summer 1946

'WITHOUT HAVING KNOWN YOU...'

Without having known you but as the light in their eyes,
The shape contrived with many flashes
As a cut stone has, conjured with love and wishes,
To be illuminated further by the reflected rays
Of its own shimmer and shifting come from these eyes –
Without having known you but having grown
Friendly and more, including always your bright name
Among those I would choose to die with
In the moment when the ring of fire dies down –
Our meeting was only the meeting of two ghosts,

Fingering glass, missing the good way in,
Hearing old echoes of the mediums who were our hosts,
Waiting cold and still for the séance to begin.

THE LONELY COMPANY

No explanation blew a wider gate
Than finding how closely carried early and late
In what I must call the heart or breast
Are the bright figures of the just,
Those who, since the first splash of a stone,
Now, and tomorrow, are the best of us.

Born under Capricorn to be
Most criminal yet also the most free,
Who, after the mind takes them down
Into the bitter town,
Return with some weeping,
Gone soft with the gentleness of the homecoming;
The most afraid and best prepared for death
And the day of wrath.

They do not come with bombs
Yet are made unwelcome.
Above the sad-frocked and the flicker-eyed
They spike like stars.
I leave it to them, not nuns, to say my prayers,
And since this gate blew wide
Know we shall never be separated
For where they are there the heart goes along.
They are the company I would choose to die among.

FOND REBUKE FOR A GRUDGED GIFT

You who thought four-and-six too much to spend
On twenty cigarettes of Russian blend
When I sank in the ocean of my craving,
When through my blood dark nicotine ran raving
And I foresaw with agony the chill
Of riding back alone to Muswell Hill
Drowned in the breakers of my twin desire,
(Of which the greater was tobacco's fire) –
You, who declared that two pence for a smoke
Would vex th'inhaling lung and make it choke –
Would you deny the silkworm's pure belief
That inspiration winds from mulb'rry leaf?
Or snatch away the cabbage from the bite
Of all the daughters of the cabbage-white?
Hard though you be, I will not credit that
You'd separate the catmint and the cat.
How could you then disdain the passion which
Stormed, in that arid hour, for Marcovitch?
Made all my black blood leap towards the leaves
Which, like the mulb'rry to the silkworm, weaves
The fabric of my poetry, throws high
My cabbage-gotten, green-veined butterfly?
Is four-and-six too much for perfumed hours
Bought at the cost of dry Odessa's flow'rs?
Am I unworthy of such dear delight?
(Remember – nothing cheaper was in sight.)
Indulge this weakness, love, and you'll restore
My greater weakness: loving you the more.

17 June 1946

THE LOVERS

With the violence that fire-engines
Make on a Sunday town
Bolting through forests of bells,
To the blinded house in the lane,
He would make his arrivals.
But her speed was in her waiting.
He left, then returned to the one
Moment where time was gone,
The long look from the eyes,
Where each journeyed at home,
Each in his countryside,
As they stood in the jealous town.
He was gone and the birds rose,
Dusting their sound away,
And the houses cried for the moon,
As they swelled or sank in the noonday,
Then slyly crept shut their doors.
But her peace was away from them.
From over the clocks and spires
Flung the birds in a whistle of wings,
Then down to soften the stone
With the faintness of their alighting,
And he of the hundred fires
Returned to his blinded virgin.
The houses awoke on the morrow
And chattered like teeth, aware,
Of their majesties standing there,
Crowned with a proud fullness,
In a remarkable, swift stillness
In a moment without sorrow.

Modern British Writing, 1947

THE CHANGING WIND

Past my window runs a tree,
All the leaves are in my room,
A shiver of water passes over.
There is no stillness ever again.
I saw the table break in three,
I saw the walls cascading down,
I saw the hard hair of my lover
Drift out upon the flowing green.
I saw the clove dark enemy
Stare from the bed where I had lain,
I saw my face in hers to be.
There is no stillness ever again.

Sun and wind had come for me –
What is my house but a flight of wings?
A flight of leaves, a flutter of rain,
A sidelong slipping of light in rings?

And now a scream possesses me –
Too high to hear, yet can I hear it;
And now transfixed upon a pain,
Too thin to feel yet must I bear it.
– This scream, this pain, they are not mine,
Water and air is all I am,
A tree has shaken the staircase down –
Then what has rustled and entered in?

I knew the other ones had come.
I knew my heart was theirs to claim.
I felt the millions in my room.
There is no being alone again.

The Listener, 19 December 1946

ON THE BOAT

In your dreams we are on this boat.
I am in grey with a crossed stole.
It's night: brass hinges, hooks. Steps
(Something between an escalator
And a fire escape) and one of us
Gets lost in the glistening geography
(Or language) of the unearthly
Island, humming, (waiters and all)
Through the resisting wall-faces
Of the unmentionable, muscular sea.

Trip over the step to the forbidden galley
– You are forgiven! It's the magic night!
Louder the humming: voices of the dead
Forever young in the next room!

SPAIN-AND-JUNIPER

Spain-and-Juniper with downward smile, into catastrophes
Always steering, marking narrowly a point of storm;
Past the Main Chance, the Log Rollers, till all at sea is
He for whom I wake to cry alarm.

I wake with the barking dog in the dark to hear
The grind of his ship. How the curtains blow out as it
Heels in a pale blaze by, while I on the cold floor there
Must stare at black glass hiding the shipwrecking night.

For he is a rare one, a rare and dear one; seven
Sons could be split from his wits and each be greater
Than himself lets. Still he goes wooing ruin.

O Spain-and-Juniper, pain will not make you better;
Not because you are hurt will you be forgiven
But for love's sake and there is the heart of the matter.

'YOU WERE NOT HERE, YOU WERE NEVER HERE...'

You were not here, you were never here
Yet I wake with the barking dog in the dark
With the sound of your ship grinding near
The shipwrecking rock that your sombre heart
Picks out for your bred-in-the-bone undoing,
Your never-living-unless-you're-dying,
To hurt yourself and stiffen and quicken your art.

Because I love you and because I am
As much yourself as any man or woman
And because my manner of multiplicity
Encourages me in thinking it my duty
To dive to the bottom to know how the sea lives,
– (Ever after carrying salt to the ocean) –
I now have you to wake me as you cry for your loves.

GOOD FRIDAY 1947

Here we are, in the sooty garden at the back,
With winter over, and our chests tight with tears
On this Good Friday, and the first bulbs in flower.
How cold it was! Remember our candle breaths,
Our locked and bolted bones; that peg-legged climb
Through lunar landscapes up St James' Lane
To the bus-stop in the eight o'clock dark morning?
Remember the evening buses, like lighted houses,

Skidding us home to fires through banks of snow?
Let it be over, the hanging on the green hill.
Let it be Easter and a blessing for this year.

Beyond the fence, (which was twice blown down,)
Is the Chinese river of people with tables and chairs
On their shoulders, who have set out to walk for ever.
Beyond the fence the skeletons of Europe.
The bird-faced children bend to the camera-eye
A gaze so unresentful and contemplative
They might not know they starve. Oh! let it be time
For the cave to thunder forth its graveyard rock,
For love to catch the wildfire spring alight!

4 April 1947

THE SCULPTURED WOMEN OF HENRY MOORE

Lizard-headed women from the first rocks
Sitting in faceless silence in a calm
Of being nothing but a weight on the earth's weight.
Great monoliths of arching wood and stone.
Some hollowed to a sea-shell's basin for a head to rest,
Or fashioned round a space to window the moving world,
Or swelling with the whole of a hill's green side.
Caved in its dumb place sleeps the peninsular child.
Their stillness, in their charge perpetual,
Is only as still as the rotating moon.
Their age is only a planet's life. Their bones,
Born of a fire, may die with the last rock and mammal.

THE SIX JULYS OF 1947

Such a summer! Till the last December-heart melted away,
And the newspaper woman sat steaming-out on her box in
                    Kingsway,
(Wet as a rag for months she'd been) and down side streets
The heat barred your way.

Everyone went on the tops of buses, (up there you go fastest,)
You get entangled in trees and the leaves come swimming
                    against the glass,
And the drivers repay the lost minutes down Muswell Hill
                    Broadway,
Diving down; fearing nobody.

It was so warm for so long; you could lift your arms in
                    summer,
Or walk home slowly, thinking, with the dark as soft as a
                    flower,
And the moon as green as an opal and the town quiet as a
                    breath
That shows a man's alive.

It came like a gift, like good news, like a kind of forgiveness;
At first we could not accept; only the worst reassures us.
And then we gave in, and the summer swept over us, reaping
Bruised grain, poorly sown.

New Directions in Prose and Poetry, No. 10, 1948

THE KIND SOFA

Edward Rigg and Emmeline
Swam on a sofa which became
Their closest friend,
Yielding, kind,
Providing their whole needs for one
Striped, buttoned hour.
To the hanging moon
Of Edward's face she could not explain
How he set free her convict mind
To visions flashed off a knife blade,
To astonishing landscapes slitted
Through dungeon walls.
She could not tell him how she lay
Smiling to find herself pelted with white
Paper boxes, dropped deliberately
From some sensational height.

New Directions in Prose and Poetry, No. 10, 1948

JUSTICE

A theatrical agent got lost among acrobats,
His glasses fell off as he swung from the high trapeze.
Miss La Rue in her Pimlico front and back
Smiled through the pins as she walked on her knees
Round the flounces of Violet Beauchamp's second-act frock.
And Septimus Rorke, still touring the Isles of Si Pong,
(With no contract) – looked up to the sky full of trees
And crackled a laugh, as though he were young,

Or happy, or talented, or not wearing stays.
The agent had carved up the world into 'Seconds',
'Stout Character', 'Elderly Blondes'. He never returned
Photographs. He was cruel to midgets. He fell, screaming, among sea-lions.

New Directions in Prose and Poetry, No. 10, 1948

TWO DOGS OLD

Two dogs are dead, mother and son,
Both very old, in my lifetime.
Ten bird centuries are gone
And a grave-wide meadow of butterflies.

But I'll not be the oldest one,
Nor the last, and for all my doubt and shame
I shall not finally look uncommon,
And no one tell my bones from theirs.

None know the hare's foot luck at heart,
Or what it followed, and if it turned back;
When difference is over, no need to speak,
And worlds are put out, when eyes are dark.

Now, two dogs old, from the hill where I've come,
Where, for a moment, I am alone,
I can see, years off, as the mist is clearing,
Some men putting up a scaffolding.

Poetry Quarterly, Winter 1948

TIME OFF

The days rush round without me
For I have stepped aside to be ill.
You could think I lay in the deaf river bed
I am become so untroubled and still.
But I sleep in other and many streams
In sickroom lifetimes of winter mornings,
(Very young again, given a hyacinth
Whose scent grew never less) – recalling
The cold petals on my nose, the scent was
Deep as the earth. It seems to me now
I prepared to go out to a place that never was
And that childhood has no truth. I lay
Hearing the others busy, dreamed
Of an endless Christmas. All spent.
But nothing is over: to and fro
Rocks the spirit; the enchantment
Breaks back. My time is not
Yours. This is time off, to lean
To the inward, letting in what will.
Tomorrow, join you, better for being ill.

IN THE HOLIDAYS

'Find me a school here!' She hauled on five lines
And landed the harbour. Courteously returned
    The stare of the sea,
    Performed the ceremony
Of blessing its fishes with her looking. Earned
Shadows of gulls on her face. With their throat she cried:
    'Don't let me go back,
    Where are the rocks

In Muswell Hill? Oh here I fetch the milk in the morning
And in the evening, alone'. It was a blink of light in the harbour
    Stung your eyes
    Into ocean flowers.
And already the smell of the sea was the smell where the sea had been.
Rock-salt cottages grew from the harbour stone into fossils
Where you were indoors and outdoors at the same time. You were
    Always on roofs
    And always in the harbour
In a limpet light as mild as clouds, as salt as seagulls.

It was a weight of kite-shaped fish they were unloading
Shoulders gasping with baskets, hooks, it made your hands hurt
    Against the screen
    Of black ropes; bleeding;
Rasping of the dead, athletic flesh and slipping cold over the cold stone.
You could eat the fish by looking. You hooked the boats
In a tangle of eyelashes. Emily hauled in the harbour with five years.
    'May I live here?'
    'One day'. 'But I'll be *older*'.
And the gulls will no longer roar in the night like hyenas
While the heart walks under the pillow, the moonlight
    Burning your tongue
    When you are young
You are the work of wishes, living near-to, where nothing has a name.

THE THREAD

You'd think she did not love enough,
Her love is made of skinny stuff;
A cobweb.

But taut and trembling as the string
Teased by a bow on violin
Until it screams.

It has no left or right or space,
So narrow that it has no face –
Yet does not break.

One foot before the other goes,
The swaying lady – ah! she knows
That far below

They sit upon their velvet chairs
And watch in case the rope betrays
And lets her go.

Though you may laugh or sneer to see
A path so circumscribed, it's she
The courage has;

And look – the gossamer above
Still holds, beneath her dance of love,
So light she is.

THE ONLY THING TO DO

The only thing to do is to put together
       Horses with marigolds.
Awaken strangers, encourage prodigies
       In a burst of snows.
Pull the red shutters fearlessly apart,
       Visit the pit,
Collect pearls and resins, wax, webs and silk
       For one's profit,
Then yield at last a fatter birth of fruit
       Than one was able
Before the hammer threat woke up courage
       At a bare table.

CONJURORS

This crusty July, blackfly
    And other small, moist flies –
        Whiskers so thin
        They are not felt on skin –
Liking a dry July
    Interrupted the performance
    Of the opening of some flowers.

Nasturtiums' circus balance
    Of little heads and great wheels
        Went heeling sideways
        Under the puny flies'
Procession of slow advance –
    Who could be changed to grease
    By a thumb flicked over a leaf.

And as a leaf I picked
    I saw my fingers smeared with the dead
        And I hated this meek
        Giving-up of ghosts by black
Destructive pests, too quick
    To surrender their flash of daylight,
    – As if a cloud had wiped cows from a field.

Everything is eating or eaten.
    The compost heap drives its mill as
        Seeds in it sprout
        Castaway plants open out
Into the heat of the garden,
    While nasturtiums here big as umbrellas
    Wear a bright display of caterpillars,

Which have eaten between the spokes.
　　　Brisk as ponies, three abreast
　　　　　They scythe their lanes
　　　　　Through sweet and pepper greens
That chequered caterpillars make.
　　　No other leaf they like to taste;
　　　Nasturtium their nurse and hostess.

Transparent as your eyelid
　　　Is this tender leaf's skin,
　　　　　It holds no reflection
　　　　　Yet in the sun's direction
Is seen, in health, glittered
　　　With the tips of a pin
　　　That fade at the first bruising.

Green ivory the stalk
　　　Snapping with rich oils
　　　　　That pulse and push
　　　　　To a great umbrella bush
And thrust into gravel walk
　　　Long messengers on bicycles
　　　Balancing umbrellas at right-angles.

Of such juices are made caterpillars.
　　　I put seven in a tray
　　　　　With a window of glass
　　　　　To watch them ripple past,
Scything from the edges
　　　Of seven round leaves a day
　　　And growing – until the 28th of July.

Chosen as conjurors and given
    Cells that bloom like water flowers,
        They do not play
        But heartily try
To prove with perfect conjuring
    Dear life, if dear enough, allows
    A blind dive into a hatful of shadows.

They ate no more. A whisper told
    Them: 'Caterpillars, all begin!'
        Through the night
        They dryly ran about
Until one spun a puff of mould
    To fix his end on, then, to plan,
    He spat a thread to fix him upside down.

Doubled back he spat
    And spun thirty threads in one
        Till he lay within a loop
        Tethered over his fourth hoop,
This thread to keep off bird or rat
    Or the wind or houses falling down,
    For he would melt and hope to live again.

Now all the bright ponies are still
    From Highgate to Angmering,
        For three days wait
        Heads bent in a praying shape,
Contracted and stiffened until
    They recede from the surface dizzily, with pain,
    At speed they take leave of their eyes, legs, brain.

Something has so altered in the night,
        Surely the wind changed to make this?
                The racking caterpillar gone
                And a pale nymph lightly borne
Under the old thread. Might
        It be a ghost? The mask on its face
        Has a beak of gold. It is like a little fish!

It is like a waxen fish
        Filled with green leaves
                With a veiny hint
                Of two wings' imprint,
With a waist, with a twitch-
        Ing tail, with a sheaf
        Of yellow dots. It is hooded like a witch.

It has come among us hooded
        And it has no bones!
                It cannot walk
                It wears a long cloak
But is also naked;
        It is the skin round albumen,
        The caul, the bag about the yolk.

It is nothing but a bud
        Too late for the spring,
                It will wither away
                It will never be a flower,
It will shrink without food,
        It is a vegetable swelling,
        A cyst, a nodule that grew one morning.

It is just a bit of dirt,
　　　　It never grew at all,
　　　　　　　The dropping of a hen
　　　　　　　Got in from the garden,
It will smooth itself out
　　　　　Like a table, like a floor, the material
　　　　　Of houses; it will spread into a wall.

Oh I cannot make it go
　　　　Though I kill it with my eyes.
　　　　　　　It's a castle of glass
　　　　　　　It's a door I cannot pass
It's a hill of snow
　　　　　It's an aviary wrapping round the skies,
　　　　　It's an aquarium; it's a bed for butterflies.

I have been a stalk, a leaf,
　　　　A grub, a fish with beak of gold.
　　　　　　　I fear the dark
　　　　　　　With a double knock
And I hate intruders – that's the truth.
　　　　　And here's the truth: I am half dazzled
　　　　　By a fancy, violent and old.

Leave a frog and find a dove,
　　　　Find a dish of blackberries
　　　　　　　Where a snake crept,
　　　　　　　Find an owl in a cobweb
Where a hare slept. Improve
　　　　　On these – no metamorphosis
　　　　　Awful as caterpillar to chrysalis.

Stare till you've insects in your eyes,
      To see will not this trick explain:
           Head in two
           Nymph bursting through,
Legs and face but worn-out clothes,
      Handsome skin rolled to a hairy grain
      By the faceless babe it could not contain.

A hairy grain is all I spy
      Of the caterpillar proud
           In his carpet coat
           Who so lovingly ate
The burning juices of July;
      Who spun his noose and cast his shroud
      And slept on the groundsheet of the dead.

Unborn are the butterflies of the south
      And the caterpillars gone.
           Images of August
           Are carried in these chaste
Cases which have no mouth
      To lap the rivers of the beans
      Tumbling up out of the ground,

Or touch the peas' cool paste.
      Filled with the dying and the growing in the wrath
           Of their commission
           To achieve transfusion,
Then I can break but not awake,
      Nor hurry that congealing drop of breath
      To build myself one butterfly on earth.

As a face at window palely pressed
        Moves, leaving the glass dark,
            So now this bottle
            Darkens, though a full
Rigged ship awaits tomorrow's test
        Of spindle spars and stays. The clock
        Tells fourteen days have passed in the ark.

Fourteen days, and then a crack!
        A skull-grey face with tendril-coiled
            Antennae; wet
            Wings, in folds yet
Of greenish gold with spots of black,
        And a grey fur back, walk like a child
        Unbalancedly into the world.

The involutions of her early wings
        Invite a finger's cruelty
            To know the damp
            Place where she once dwelt,
Or to deface and itself win
        From each cold hollow, guiltily,
        Some of the dews and dustings of her beauty.

She walks like a boat on the beach
        Dragging her drying sails,
            While the last
            Memory of her past
Shakes from her tail: a bead
        Of amber dew, unnoticed as the shell
        That husked and housed her in its brittle walls.

Climber of curtains, long she'll not hang there;
        Taut are her wings and head-dress.
                She will feed on sweet
                Slippets but will never eat.
She will find her answering angel in the air.
        She will not lay her eggs upon nasturtiums' crease
        And will not remember the taste of the leaf.

Suddenly she is soundlessly flapping across the broad
        Floor of the air without a trial;
                The sun takes her
                Across to the blue buddleia.
Out of her depths in air she is not afraid.
        When she reaches the tree she finds it full
        Of her own shapes and becomes indistinguishable.

NIJINSKY

He stopped getting older this new-born April,
Nijinsky, veiled and beautiful with fame,
We buried him long and long before this funeral
But a room still changes at the sound of his name.
He used such stuff that is always dying –
Flesh and bone, flesh and bone,
He who was all our dreams of flying
In air, is stiffened to a straight stone;
Five long tendons bent like a bird's
Are got by the frost, are feet of stone.

Wild and far as wolves began the story
With a tumbling troupe in Russia and one who
Sent up a ball and lost it in the sky,

Careering after to catch it his life through.
One child apprentice from an old stock,
Trimmed to his fathers in Imperial dress
Who crossed some spell-bound river in the dark
Where his dance flickered with a blinding tenderness.
'I am a rhyme' he said, 'I dance my singing,'
'I will build a dam in Russia.' He built one in space.

Down through a pin of light to Petersburg
The changeling brother we have never seen
Floats on our held breath; a nakedness
Spinning its dumb music where a man had been.
The ragged petals of the Rose of death
Furl round harsh muscle – we remember
He had the strength could have made him a blacksmith,
This Faun, this Ghost, this young and mortal dancer ...
These eyes like wings, this bow-and-arrow face
Are only tilted shadows on a page.

ROETHKE

I like Roethke (pronounced Retke)
I don't know him; I like his poems;
I like the poet who wrote them. He
Moves among his poems as familiarly
And as gracefully, as in his greenhouse:
Watches his poems grow admiringly
As his bulbs and orchids. Like a painter
Sometimes he writes what he sees and sometimes
With the surest step, steps across the stepping-stones of his mind –
A strange country to us – but we leap with him
From flat round stone to stone and we don't fall in.
On each round stone he writes a dream
And the black water swirls in between.

A MAN IN THE GARDEN

I think there's a man in the garden,
In a raincoat like sodden leaves.
I can see him from the attic window;
He did not walk in; I think he appeared,
Or else he is there to complete the garden
Which, at this time of year is broken stalks,
Stringy creepers, things I had not tied up, swaying.
To complete the garden by being a man, as though
A man should stand in every garden.

His face is twilight-coloured, his hair dark
Too long, unbrushed, a tramp's hair, yet
I can't see properly, but am filling him in,
Like pictures in fire or fog or ghosts in the curtains.

He looks about, up at the empty plum tree,
To the old coarse snow still lying in hollows,
At the bent black of stumps, the broken stems
Of rose bushes after a hard winter. He looks in a certain way:
Not curiously, or with understanding, or with feeling;
But like an observer in a strange land, set down suddenly
Unable to relate what he sees to what he has seen before.
I'm sure of this: he is a man without a garden of his own.

He is an idea of a man; middle-aged, worn, meek of body,
With low-instepped, un-beautiful, long, middle-aged feet –
Like the feet of Zeus with his thunderbolt (carved from such a man)
And thin, white arms that change colour at the hands.
It is a privilege to be human; and to be man, or a woman.
It is a privilege to be middle-aged, and to stand in a garden,
Or even to stand at all.

SEMINAR AT BRUSSELS, JANUARY 1963

Thin, thin were the trees and trellises of the Rue Royale
In a thin and thready wind full of salt and snow
That had bullyingly rolled across the continent from Moscow
To whip us with the tail-end of its rope as it trailed home.

Thin and mean was the black-and-white of the snow in the streets;
Thin the streaks of the snow on the right-angled trellises,
And the snow-greasy flags and cobbles of Brussels,
Leading to spires and the undeniable landscapes of Breughel.

And all along the grey, interminable Rue Royale
Between the office blocks, were the Napoleonic
The beautiful facades of the shuttered and classic
Flat-faced, thin-slatted, grey-shuttered 'hôtels'.

Fringing the Gardens opposite, this trellis, like a train,
A trellis of trained trees, thin, mean and rectangled,
(That would, in the summer, grow tangled into green)
– This trellis moved beside us like a slow old train.

Hot with baked air the hotel rooms and the lecture rooms:
(The great greenhouse of a hotel, nineteen-eight, fake Versailles,
The brain-washing offices, seductively comfortable and sly) –
Hot with baked air was the public indoors of cold Brussels.

In the hot, baked air of the lecture hall corridor
We read in the English papers Hugh Gaitskell was being killed
Inch by inch, by a virus. Inch by inch we shuffled
Back to the Seminar. Time had stopped for one and all.

*****

Time had stopped in Brussels in the Rue Royale.
De Gaulle had said 'Non!'; Gaitskell was finally killed.
And the hot cornucopias of our hotel
Remembered a time when the foyer was full.

And the ladies and gentlemen went out one morning
To see the great room of Waterloo
And returned for luncheon. It is now empty at luncheon,
The glass roof is dingy and grey and the groups of sofas have nothing to do.

FEBRUARY

February, February ... soft is the sound
       Of the name of the month at the end of the winter.
       Blind as a chrysalis; confused in its weather,
It puts buds on the lilac and ice in the ground.

In February, February, in the war,
       In the night, with lights and nurses, I had a daughter.
       I, who was a daughter, was now a mother;
That is what I remember February for.

DEATH IN LYNDALE AVENUE

Step-laddered to where I can't
       Be my own compasses, I
       Measure the years ahead by
The white windows I'll paint.

Doors, walls, ceilings, all –
       Year after year I've snow-stormed over,
       Though each spring stiffer, the spring fever
Jerks me where white flakes fall

Round my hot head. Yesterday,
        In this fanatical fix, breathing
        Not sweet spring but paint, saw a coffin
Out of next door as I bobbed in my bay

Window. Saw the black cloth
        Lopsidedly drape it, and two little nurses
        Follow my neighbour, with child faces
Modestly down the pink path,

Bend through the double doors and wait
        (Politely not talking) for the mortuary team
        To settle in, and the broad-beamed
Glittering black car to start.

So departed, in home-made fashion,
        My right-hand wall, and her dreams of rats
        Climbing up lavatories; her kindness to cats:
A gardener; passionate old Jewish woman.

Death dared fell her, or else she chose
        To leave the new apple tree grow by itself;
        To let go and drift, feet first
Away from her lace-curtained house

And the few left who knew her with love –
        In full view of a girl in trousers
        Washing a car, a man pruning roses,
And myself, crossing another spring off.

April 1963

'SO LONG AGO I'D READ THE BOOK...'

So long ago I'd read the book
I'd lost the images I'd made,
And when I trod that print again,
New images were overlaid.
Then suddenly the old came back –
A double depth, a place-on-place;
And I can never make them one,
Or see which is the brighter face.

So like, yet unlike this, with you
My love: there were no years between
The first you and the second you –
One hour, no more, had raised a screen
Between the two of you. A gift
Had touched us like a flash of fire:
Apollo stood before the screen,
And all behind it was a liar.

'I HAD KNOWN HIM BABIES AGO...'

I had known him babies ago
To speak to – coldly. Did not know
His face had locked and said goodbye
To the rainbow.

Stiff-necked, I thought; he'd turned
Towards ambition; had not learned
We could give more than *they*,
Were he a friend.

Better than no bread,
He had hoped for half a loaf, he said,
(This was babies later) – but half-alive
Is half-dead.

So he made sons to go
After the long-lost rainbow;
Was tender, not stiff-necked to them,
And let them grow

As he had not been let: no tree
Umbrella'd over him yet left him free.
Trained like a race horse, he submitted blindly,
But win or lose were both unkindly,
And a locked face cannot see.

'NOW I CAN LOVE YOU AGAIN...'

Now I can love you again, now we are parting,
My Siamese twin, my old, mad, faery father:
My essence of all the good in all the men
Who lived or wrote poetry; my strange and darling husband.

My opponent, friction, the enemy in my house:
The crying inside the walls, the only one
I could never influence: who strolled in, who influenced me,
Who struck and stuck to me – the astonished host.

Now you are going as lightly as you came
Your cardboard suitcases tied up with string
Years and years of me in them; yet they contain
No more than they brought, in 1949.

'HOW CAN I USE THIS LOVE YOU DO NOT KNOW OF?'

How can I use this love you do not know of?
How stop unworthy daydreams? Daydreams are only
        A dream of drinking in a thirsty sleep:
        A baby's dummy: a rubber doll the lonely
Take to their cold beds instead of love.
            'Where you sow, do not expect to reap.'

'You reap where you did not sow.' I know this is true:
That nothing is wasted, least of all, loving.
            Thankful, indeed, for a heart that can feel pain,
        And thankful to still feel sexual craving,
And thankful to find I am as alive as you,
            And thankful to you for bringing me alive again.

LIGHTNESS

I take less space; liking lightness
Am glad to be lighter. Can jump higher;
Dream I jump like a flea, giddy at
The kiss of the ceiling.
(Not flying – jumping.) The cat
Dreams that it flies. The bird
Dreams it flies faster. The flea
Dreams of blood and bedclothes.

(As strong, the flea, as a safety pin;
It pulls chariots, works machines.
Tried out for another planet, it
Is wasted here; a misfit.)

Curl up in a corner of the car,
Narrow-bottomed. Swoon

Slowly down. Lie on your lover
Light as a counterpane.
Flat-bellied, withered-breasted,
Salad-fed, light-of-head,
Jump! Jump! Jump!

'THREE NUNS WALKED IN REGENTS PARK...'

Three nuns walked in Regents Park
In a wind that whipped their veils sideways.
Like ragged birds, so tall and dark,
Black leaves, or ragged scarecrows.

Flat-footed moved; three ragged brush-strokes.
I followed, yet they moved much softer;
By the autumn wind were they made a joke of?
No – they were shaken with laughter.

TO A SICK FRIEND

This cubist weather
Falls about
Like diced bacon
From the sky.
You are ill and tethered by
A lack of fuel in the flesh.
Through the shopping,
Through the gin,
Through the egg I boiled in anger
(Eating only not to die)
Rain your golden coins of skin
And your salty cubes of flesh.

A Charles X chair with outstretched arms
Stands still against the racing house.
The racing street is cubed and cut
By fly's-eye lenses of the glass.
Fur-muffled, whistling, breathes a cat,
Wasting its short and different time.

Oh different indeed are all times that
Burst their banks one winter day.
Held what we could as we swept by,
Croaked 'courage!' – by telepathy
Heard 'courage, courage!' down the flooded street.

UNINTERESTING SONNET

I am indeed in the shallows of today,
Yesterday broken behind me, tomorrow taken away,
And the salt gone out of the sea, the water flat
And my sight dull as a fish and no bait.
Blind in my right eye as in my dream;
I am my ill mother and all that has been
In her triumphing youth is smashed. And I
Am my old and disappointed father whose right eye
Too, was blind in another way. I cannot mourn
Them, for they never were; nor claim
Tragedy in their romantic deaths. I face
My unromantic, casual origin; the less
Because they're less; dead as they died,
Dull as they're dull, without love left or pride.

CINEMA

The world's like a film on the eyeball
Pretending to make sense;
Half he controls, he's half in thrall
To that iridescence.

The world unravels like a spool
At the back of his mind,
Projecting, so his eye is fooled,
Illusory humankind

On a screen with which his mind confers
From its throne of plush;
Strangers, love- and hate-like words
In solipsistic hush.

Until when the fairy-lights blink on
And the national anthem's played,
Dreamily he faces the dark alone,
King of all his days.

THE ALTRUIST

After the spaciousness of alcohol
And the rich, visionary smokes,
Afflatus-fires gone cool,
And the unctuous phallic jokes,

The disputants solipsise.
But she, with glad alacrity,
Looks honey-eyed into their eyes,
Surmising each integrity.

What impersonal themes
Goaded them into the small hours?
Power, morality, sexual dreams?
Insinuation is her power,

Protesting innocence, to intuit
Their enslavement to desire;
But always, under the lady's foot
A crushed snake retires.

Dawns, and they must say goodbye
Whom she cannot hate,
Swaggering their lonely ways,
Sententious and inadequate.

TWO ELEMENTS

She's fine, albeit guarded
Whose dainty fingers trimmed my incandescence
To a drawing-room flame, then disregarded
What I could ill afford; this evanescence

Into something oozier, ill-thought-of,
For I leave too many traces.
I was gauche; I couldn't prove
The fineness of my flame against her graces.

Now she flames in beautiful mistrust
(My name is mud) pretending not to see me.
Should I extend a hand though crack and crust?
We were elemented differently.

MENDEL'S GARDEN

So we go on, the iron papers,
Appropriating starry fields
To reckon under roof, keepers
Of the old, statistical yields,

Late workers in planetary light,
Compounded of the same blue clay
In which we love and fight
And dream blue nights away,

Eugenists of efflorescence
Culturing our nightmare city
With iron gnashings, brokerage, pence,
Wanting a monk's serenity.

Old scientists, so we go on,
Stumbling upon nothingness
Late in life, all floor gone
On which to kneel and make redress.

LETTERS

49 Cholmeley Crescent N6
8 July 1944

Dear David,

It is in the evening: I am in bed. Beni is fiddling uncertainly about the room. Sydney is having a drink with Peggy Jean at the Wheatsheaf. A pink light from the sunset behind the house is on the sky outside. The sirens have gone but there is quietness. (And now not any more: a bumbling P. Bomb is about, somewhere.) I have a feeling about you that it would be a loss not to tell you, that you have come comfortingly into my life as a strength. I know that this is neither a glamorous or perhaps even welcome kind of compliment, and I am not putting down now any other kind, purposely, but the point of writing that one is that you might not have guessed it. I have minded not having your country address, and the weekend feels more perilous because of that. Mostly I have found the rocks to be boring and the charmers to be sandy, and it really is lovely to have a gentle and imaginative rock at half an hour's distance.

You know I believe deeply in spontaneity, sincerity &, where possible, candour, & no tricks; so believing this it would be a needless loss not to tell you that I have that absolute certain happy feeling about you that you will never not be in my life, somewhere, and that it has been great gain to have met you. You will know me well enough now to read no more and no less than what I write in words. There is no invisible ink between my lines.

Maurice Lindsay has organised a poetry evening at which Sydney & I have each been asked to read poems. It is on Friday at, I think 5. At first I said no, because of the almost-decided weekend at your mama's, then I thought it would be a Good

Thing to meet Lindsay & the poetry blokes, so I have said yes, if I can get Emily looked after at that time: at this moment I cannot think of any one able to look after her, so nothing is settled. Until about 3 days ago I was not especially nervous at the raids, & slept well all nights but one: then together came Churchill's speech, the ceiling falling and Beni's constant tension and jumpiness and near-panic, not to mention his compulsion-neurosis-song that he is forced to sing in his head night and day, and all this has made me very worried at the P. Bombs. He just will not go out of the room, even when Sydney was in bed, and we both wanted early sleep. Yet I have a soft spot for Beni and can be very glad of his company for hours together.

The one night before when I did not sleep well it was because of a fear of being killed in my sleep! So of course this kept me awake. But during a short time of sleep I had such a long, intricate & clear semi-nightmare dream that on waking at a bomb crash I got up and wrote it down, taking an hour and a half, & totally able to ignore the near P. Planes. This I have since elaborated into a 4,000 word story. (But nothing is added to the dream). This now needs re-writing, and I am going to try to write more interestingly, as you suggested. Sydney likes my story-writing style but urges me to experiment more with words.

II

I have been aiming hitherto at a style both formal and economical: partly in the belief that such an unemotional bare-bones structure is the best background for a coloured and unusual story, and where horror is concerned it is almost a technical trick. I was impressed by Hugh Kingsmill's use of it, & Richard Hughes, & I. Compton-Burnett and Henry James. (Although I admit that they write perfectly & with a knowledge of grammar & style that I am still very slowly beginning to gather in.) (This letter has been thrice interrupted by the scramblings of Beni & me down the stairs, into Emily's room, and then rather sheepishly, up the stairs, back to our posts, I in my bed with the inkpot on the wireless, Beni reading my new copy of 'Scottish Art & Letters'). (Not a very good 5/- worth, this, a bloody awful cover by J.D. Fergusson, & nothing very exciting inside save a poem by Sydney, almost his best, that ends: –

'... no, I'll inherit
No keening in my mountainhead or sea,
Nor fret for few who die before I do.'
['Many Without Elegy']

These lines are to be quoted by William Montgomerie in an article on dead Soutar. They have a profound braveness I think and are incidentally an important part of Sydney's philosophy.)

David Archer & my pen-pal Chuck & Sydney & Beni have been here today, what a lot of people. Your roses have dropped. It has become a symbolic phrase now – 'to collect your roses.' Thus will I always word an invitation to you.

Sydney has just come in, very tight.

Next Morning. A lot of bombs this morning: one came on a long glide, beginning by being just a buzzer in the far off distance & stopping so we thought it wd land on Kensington, & then gliding half across London towards us till its glide got very loud & we dashed downstairs. It exploded a street away on a tenement. More of our ceiling came in and my great Highgate friends, Mary & Cecil Stewart rang up to say their flat was quite wrecked & they both cut. We started to go round to them, all the streets full of glass & cut people &

ambulances, but Mary came running out with blood on her to say not to come, no place for babies and other friends were there helping. So we came back, & here we are, the bombs still coming, and us all a bit shaken. A warden came round to ask how we were & I said cd we have a Morrison shelter & he said yes if I applied; it wd be £9. (But maybe, he added, free, if my income was below a certain level.)

Johnnie Minton is coming round at 4. Sydney & Beni are sitting around reading about sex and all the meals are lying about unwashed with bits of ceiling among them. So I must bustle myself for the honour of my flat. I will first write you out a poem that has been accepted for 'Voices' ['Superstition'].

49 Cholmeley Crescent N6
15 July 1944

David, yesterday Sydney & I set off for the poetry place which turned out to be The Poetry Society. We arrived a little later than we meant & asked in the foyer for Maurice Lindsay. An old dowdy woman in green jersey cloth was sharp with us & suspicious: 'What do you want him for? Do you know him?' 'Yes,' said Sydney, 'I know him quite well.' 'You'd better wait, I'm busy now,' said the woman, disliking Sydney's dirty unsocked ankles. 'We'll go upstairs & look for him, eh?' said Sydney & we started up when the woman stopped us by waving a wooden box. 'You can't go upstairs without putting something into the collection,' she shouted. It was annoying, but we paused, & Sydney pulled out three pence halfpenny – all his money – & tried to put it in the box. But the woman snatched it back

& said: 'Coppers! This is a silver collection!' 'That is all the money I have at all,' said Sydney. 'Oh get upstairs then,' shouted the woman – all this in front of the audience-people starting to come in. We went up and passed an open room full of old rich women sitting, and asked for Lindsay: a man said we must wait in the 'audience-chamber'. We did not, but went further up, to where another man was. I asked him if I could wash my hands. He got up very angry & shouted 'This is not a lavatory, this is The Poetry Society, there is nowhere here.' The old women in the audience room could hear all this, and I was upset altogether, & Sydney & I went out, past the collection box, and out. We went to Hazel Pynegar's office, only a street away, & I went to the lavatory, & then Hazel came back with us to the meeting. In the foyer an old man met us: 'You are very late,' he said, 'Mr Lindsay has been looking for you everywhere.'

We all went into the Audience Chamber, & Lindsay and some young man & Sydney & I were on a row of chairs facing the old women. They were terrible, dried old bones in mauve velvet hats. One man like Lord Lonsdale was there but he slept all the time. The young man like a neat little snake read an introduction. When he came to us it was like this: 'Also we have – er – Mr Graham, who has, er, published one book of poems.' Long pause. 'And er – Miss Orde will read a poem.' Lindsay then read in a weak voice a very dreary and weak talk on Scottish poetry which was mainly a list of names for the old ladies to take down in their notebooks. He mentioned the poets of the Apocalyptic school, included Sydney among the names. He rounded off his paper thus: 'But the proof of the pudding is in the eating, so here are some bits of pudding.' Meaning, the readers reading poems. Sydney, despite nervousness & obvious fed-upness, read well, as did I. Lindsay was inaudible & bad. So we dreared on. The old bones in front clapped by mistake in the middle of poems and forgot to clap at the end. The only one that made the faintest feeling of stir was a short Soutar doric poem. One heard them murmur: '... oh sweet ... charming ...' Sydney's own 'Many Without Elegy' fell entirely flat. The utter wash-outness of the whole affair was palpable to everyone, nor was it helped by the neat snake's bright winding-up of the proceedings, using words as: 'An extraordinarily interesting & exciting hour, with unique ...' etc. We on the platform were thinking of moving out when to our surprise some of the bones spoke – questions were asked, such as: 'I once saw a statue of a poet in Edinburgh – now who could that be now?'

One, in ermine, wanted the dialect poem translated. 'But I did not understand a word of it,' she said, when Lindsay declined, 'No, please do.' Suddenly we realised that they all came to the meetings & paid their money, & were not a bit diffident. It was their Poetry Society, & they could, if they liked, insist on having their questions answered. Another said: 'If the best English is spoken in Inverness why are the best poets not Scottish?' Etc. etc.

A thin old red faced white headed man at the back – like a gran'pop in an American film – got up & spoke very loudly & long, beginning: 'You say MacDiarmid is the leading Scottish poet, well to my mind he's a very uneven writer, a lot of his stuff is just so much balderdash (etc.) now why haven't you included any poems by Soutar?' – (We had – two.) – 'Soutar was – etc.', ending, 'Now that Soutar's dead something must be done for Soutar.' Then he talked on, and among things he said: 'This Hopkins you mentioned, – the trouble with Hopkins was he didn't understand his own sprung rhythm. As for these so-called poets of the New Apocalypse? Look up Matthew etc., John etc. Now G.K. Chesterton was an Apocalyptic poet, but these young men don't know about the rules of rhythm, they're just trying to draw attention to themselves ...' etc. etc. He was spluttery, & got the word 'Apocalypse' wrong each time – 'Apocalpycops' etc. I almost got the giggles, Sydney did once. He obviously did not realise, or remember, that Sydney had been introduced as such a poet. Some of the bones cottoned on, & the atmosphere was of embarrassment. The old man, I believe, was Herbert Palmer.

The whole room from the beginning had been supremely aware of Sydney's no tie or socks or handkerchief, of his air of sweaty anarchy. He hated facing such an audience, & being stared at like an okapi or something. But Palmer's attack roused him, and he suddenly started an excellent, well-worded & very emphatic exposition of 'The rules of rhythm.' Lindsay, fearing the suddenly virile atmosphere, interrupted him & the meeting was over.

* I wrote that lying on my bed being drawn by John Minton. Then a knock came at the door and a girl bustled in whom I had not seen for 2 years – a prize bore, poor girl, from Glasgow. She is out this minute to get cigarettes and at the next asterisk she will have returned. Her coming was unfortunately the cue for John Minton's leaving. She has already talked of coming 'often', 'on spec' etc. I shall be dogged by her I can see. * This morning a most extraordinary incident happened: David Archer had rung up to ask if he could borrow £5. I said yes, being sorry, as he already owes me one pound from a week ago. He said he would be round early to collect the cheque so as to get to the bank in Chelsea in time to cash it. Sydney, on hearing this, warned me that I would never get it back, & I began to feel very uncomfortable. Anyway, by 11.30 David had not come so I went out to do the shopping with Sydney, thinking he was not coming as he would never get to Chelsea in time. When we got back he was there, meeting us white lipped, as they say in books, with fury, and screaming at me – well that's a fucking silly thing to do, not to leave the cheque with Beni for me, etc. etc. Upstairs I asked him if he was <u>sure</u>

I would get it back as I cd not afford to lose it. At this he was so angry, taking the line that how <u>dare</u> I not trust him, he shouted at me so loud that Emily burst into tears; he strode & fussed about the room after me gabbling & yelling that he <u>had to have</u> the money and how dare I not get it to him in time, bloody buggering people who wouldn't trust him – '<u>No one</u> trusts me,' he shouted, 'John Singer goes about saying I didn't pay him back the £5 he lent me – and I <u>won't</u> pay him back now, for that – there isn't one shop that'll cash a cheque for me ...' Shakily I had written the cheque, determined on dignity, he shouted, pocketing it, 'What the bloody hell is the good of this NOW – you'll have to give me a pound as well – I <u>know</u> you've got money in the bank,' – so I did give him a pound as well. He walked about, simmering down but still at intervals shouting to justify himself. I was a bit tired and feeling sick as it happened, & Beni & Sydney were concocting a luncheon in the kitchen, & Emily howling for her separate luncheon, & now it appeared that David, who cannot resist food, however much he has eaten just before, was to stay as well. His swearing at me had made me shiver and shake, and when at one moment I was alone, & then only Sydney came in I cried and said David was not to stay to luncheon & he was never to come back. Sydney asked David to go away and David came in & made a very strange sort of apology but while doing it worked himself up into a rage again so it was the same. Finally he went saying he would pay me back the '£5' – (forgetting so soon it was £7!) – in a month.

Christine sat up talking without a break till 1 o'clock. Sydney came in drunk & went to bed, & she slept in your bed. I was sorry that she stayed because her whole talk is gossip, mostly untrue, & she had not known before about Sydney & me. She is so insensitive that she never stops to find out if she is gossiping about one's dearest friend, and a lot of her talk was about Sydney. I imagined her this morning revolving in her head the things she had told me about Sydney, including quite dull remarks such as: 'I should show him a poem of yours Julian, his judgment is fairly sound on the whole – well as I was saying about so-and-so's abortion ...'

Sydney is a bit sick & fed up today, Beni for once not here, the day looked like to be our own when Chuck – (soldier pen-pal) – turned up, & is here while I'm writing, and someone else, Patrick Rose, rang to say he was coming ... doggedly I have been writing this letter through them all, but now I must stop and clear away and be friendly. Chuck brought some cakes and Sydney has turned him onto typing a poem on Mr Weiss's capital-letter typewriter. Now Sydney is sitting beside me at the writing table – like a duet – and says he is writing a poem for Horizon. The P. Bombs were over us in the night last night again. I hope you will not spend Monday in a little cell. I could write a poem myself this minute I believe. Talking, & thinking so much makes one want to. Sydney liked the story you liked Three First Acts. That is all now. Julian Orde.

JULIAN ORDE TO DAVID WRIGHT, 15 DECEMBER 1968

38 Lyndale Avenue N.W.2.
15 December 1968

My Dear David,
How tiresome of you to write me a lovely long letter and not to post it!

But I'm very glad to have yesterday's one. I think I owed you one: did I finally say Ralph's year of birth was 1914?

Yes, I will go through the photographs and put the names of people. I gave David Abercrombie a number of Soho and other photographs, and insisted on putting the names on the backs, even though he was sure he'd remember them. I also thought to put the name of the photographer – for personal posterity!

I think the secret of making a profit out of buying books is to know where to sell them. Thank you for the tip about David A. and my Dictionary of Pronunciation. Probably the best place to go with my Tom Brown's Schooldays in Pitman shorthand is Pitman's, and the place for the maps are the map-makers ... and so on.

I'm very glad about your paper. It seems surprising that you were the first man to speak about deafness, in public, from experience – but the more marvellous that you did it. I have always thought you the undeafest deaf man I've ever met. I remember the first time we met – I didn't know you were deaf for an hour or two, and then only because someone (Sydney?) mentioned it to me. But I didn't mean just that, when I said the undeafest man. I mean the most un-cut-off, for one thing, and, for another, that you seem as aware of sound, of rhythm, and of common speech as any one – more so than most hearing people. I remember you once saying, of a word in a poem, "Air" is such a long word ...' Of course you were right, but when I've quoted this hearing people, insensitive to pronunciation (if that's the right word) have said: 'Nonsense, it's only one syllable!' I don't understand how you knew it's a long word, because one dwells on the vowels, but you did. Did you know that that extremely long word in England: 'Moon' becomes a short word in Scotland – 'M-n' and that the short word in England 'Foot' becomes long in Scotland: 'F-o-o-t'? (In fact, they pronounce it as we pronounce Moon).

But it's not just this interest in the sound of words, I think it's your colloquialness, your au-faitness with the latest jokes and phrases and words that makes it difficult to remember you're deaf. The only thing that I notice – and as a matter of fact this applies to insensitive hearing people too – is that you don't (naturally) 'hear' furniture. You might put a glass down on a table more strongly than a hearing person, not guided by the clash, or sit in a chair heavily, not hearing the creak ...

Your detachment makes it possible to write that, without fear of wounding.

I work so hard, so long, and at so many things. My job mainly, but I've usually several freelance things on – jobs for *Which?* magazine, ranging from testing to being on panels, or reviewing; marking exam papers; the odd painting commission; and recently I've become very involved with Art Schools and students, and sit on Committees, and have even undertaken to organise advertising courses and projects which may lead me to have to be a visiting lecturer at Art Colleges all over England. I met the most militant element of Hornsey Art School, along with colleagues of mine, and soon realised that I was the only real sympathiser. I've also had discussions with Ealing Students and various Principals, and am still baffled to find that I am the only grown-up who understands what the students are talking about. (I don't mean the only grown-up in England who understands, but in what ever galère I'm in.) I suppose this is partly because I've never stopped being secretly a rebel, and partly because I interview about five young people a day for jobs (in copywriting). I find it as easy to understand their point of view as for R.D. Laing to empathise with a Schizophrenic.

I'm slowly getting to the point that I can see myself not doing anything about Ralph's anthology – just putting it off, thinking I will have time sometime, when I clearly do not. It's good, in a way, not to have time, but also frightening.

It's a pity he didn't finish his index, because it's the only thing holding up an attempt at publication. There is also the problem of sorting out the apparently 'final' version from the earlier ones, and judging how nearly finished it was. Close friends of his might feel sure that he would have included other poems, if he had not died, and add them.

The effect of the handwriting, and the choice, is as though he had written them all. I find it intensely moving.

There are also masses of pamphlets, magazines, and things

bought for eventual selling, like putting down wine. I keep Meaning to do Something about sorting them out – not necessarily actually selling anything – but at least having a clear idea where everything is, but time goes by, and I get no further than sitting in a dream, reading an old magazine.

I'm very glad about your book. I refuse to sympathise about your being chained to the typewriter. I hope it's absolutely outspoken, emotionally; as well as technically enthralling. Spare no pains. Nor spare yourself. There has never been another, as far as I know, on the subject. Spare no one's feelings; be honester than you like to.

I like The Hotel as a title very much (just possibly Hotel in Amsterdam is against it). I think Nerve Ends is a rotten title. It sounds horribly "sensitive" and I don't like the idea of the cover. Also, it's not very memorable. Please change it at once. A concrete title is best, and though you may think Nerve Ends is 'concrete' I don't agree. I'm a copywriter; I know about titles and headlines. Colours are always good, incidentally – particularly for plays. (The Green Hat (book) Green for Danger, Pink String and Sealing Wax ...)

Emily was a Mouse (a small part) in Toad of Toad Hall, in London.

I was very bucked about my poem in the Penguin. I wrote to Ralph about it and asked if he had engineered it, but he hadn't. (He was always cross with you for leaving me out of yours, and including Potts!) I've never met Skelton. I must congratulate him. It seems quite a good-value book for five bob, and has become my favourite Christmas present!

I wish the poem didn't have so many bad lines in; I found it impossible to alter them, so many years later.

love to you both

Julian

‘ALL IN THE ONE NUMBER, YOU ME AND J’:
THE POETRY OF JULIAN ORDE

'A Great-Grandfather in the Battle of Waterloo'

Early in their friendship, in a letter to his mother in July 1944, David Wright reports an exchange with Julian Orde:

Me:	I had a great-uncle in the Battle of Waterloo.
Julian:	I had a great-grandfather in the Battle of Waterloo, too.
Me:	He was wounded in the leg or something.
Julian:	What was your great-uncle's name?
Me:	Murray. What was your great-grandfather's name?
Julian:	Wellesley.
Me:	Well, what did he do in the Battle of Waterloo?
Julian:	He won it. (Collapse of everybody).

Her mother, Lady Eileen Wellesley (1887–1952), was the sister of two Dukes of Wellington. On the death in 1941 of the 5th Duke, her older brother, Arthur Wellesley (1876–1941), the dukedom passed to his son, Orde's cousin, Henry Wellesley (1912–43). A captain in the Commandos, the 6th Duke was killed in Salerno, leading a charge against a German machine-gun post. Since Henry was an only son, and childless, Lady Eileen's younger brother, Lord Gerald Wellesley (1885–1972), whose estranged wife was the poet, Dorothy Wellesley, became the 7th Duke.

Before her marriage in 1916, Lady Eileen had a love affair with Rupert Brooke, 'a brief final fling', on his part, according to the *Spectator*, but his letters strike a different note: 'Eileen, there's something solid & real & wonderful about you, in a world of shadows... The time with you is the only waking hours in a life of dreams'. He sent her a gift of semi-precious stones a fortnight before his death from septicaemia in April 1915. A style icon, Lady Eileen was the subject of a portrait by E.O. Hoppé in the first number of *British Vogue* in 1916, and the National Portrait Gallery has a set of dry glass plates, four including Julian and her baby sister Jane, dated 1921. Lady Eileen's own art appears in a series of *Tatler* advertisements in 1920 for the Elspeth Phelps range of clothing, 'distinguished by taste above all criticism' (says the fashion columnist of the *Bystander*), retailed from Mayfair and a 'succès fou' with West End actresses. Rediscovered by Lucinda Gosling, they feature a gallery of 'society types', 'in a spidery and occasionally sinister style reminiscent of Aubrey Beardsley', poking fun at both advertiser and clientele, 'faintly acerbic and surprisingly self-deprecating'. In the 1930s, she was designing wallpaper and painting fabrics, but continued to paint, even when suffering from advanced multiple sclerosis. By 1944, her daughter told Wright, she had lost 'the use of her legs & hands', but 'carried on nevertheless & painted with the brush held in her mouth'.

Orde's father, Capt. Cuthbert Julian Orde (1888–1968), whose middle name had been given by family tradition to boys and girls alike for generations, was a combat pilot in WWI and the renowned portraitist of Battle of Britain aces in WWII. The family had served in the army and navy for over a century, when, in 1910, Sir Julian Orde, the poet's grandfather, secretary of the Royal Automobile Association and founder in 1904 of the Isle of Man TT Races in defiance of the mainland speed limit of 20 mph, joined the Royal Aero Club. Formed to encourage 'aero auto-mobilism and ballooning', the Club issued its first Aviators' Certificates the same year. Cuthbert Orde earned the 1914 Star, for service from the declaration of war to the First Battle of Ypres, then moved from the Army Service Corps to the Royal Flying Corps, qualifying as a pilot in 1916, with promotion, during 1917, to flight commander and captain, serving until 1919. His younger brother, Herbert Walter Julian Orde, a naval lieutenant, won the DSC in 1914 for bravery in command of a picket boat at Dar es Salaam, but was killed aged twenty-four when HMS *Goliath* was torpedoed off the Dardanelles in 1915. His elder brother, Michael Amyas Julian Orde, qualified as a pilot in 1915, but was shot down in 1916, becoming a prisoner of war for the duration. He died in a flying accident on Salisbury Plain in 1920, aged thirty-two.

Capt. Orde opened a studio in Paris in the twenties, exhibiting at the Chenil and Goupil Galleries, the Paris Salon and, in London, the Royal Academy. In 1940, he was commissioned as a war artist by the Air Ministry, spending a year on his assignment, living for a couple of weeks on almost every operational station and producing over a hundred drawings of fighter pilots selected by the squadron commander (bar one, who 'returned me the catalogue unmarked with the comment, "They're all damn' good chaps"'). *Pilots of Fighter Command: Sixty-four Portraits* was published in 1942. The 'few' include Douglas Bader, 'Cat's Eyes' Cunningham and John Drummond, still in his flight jacket, five days before he was killed. Fine, bravura portraits, certainly, but Orde's masterpiece is a 1935 portrait of his red-headed daughter, aged seventeen, in a black gown and green cloak. In amusing contrast to her languorous Renaissance arm, her face is given a rather stern look by defiant blue eyes and an aquiline, ducal nose.

Born on New Year's Eve, 1917, Julian Orde was raised in London and Paris, presented at court as a debutante and invited with her uncle, the 5th Duke, to dine at Buckingham Palace by King George V and Queen Elizabeth. The family home, 1 Durham Place, a townhouse in Chelsea, last changed hands for £8m, whilst their country mansion, Spoode House, in Edenbridge, Kent, is recorded as a monument in the Historic England Archive. Orde studied drawing at Chelsea Polytechnic, then acting at the Royal Academy of Dramatic Art. In 1937, when she was twenty, her contribution to *Time & Tide* ('… wait for no *man*'), edited by the wealthy suffragette Viscountess Rhondda, gives a glimpse of the future star-copywriter, if not also of the poet, as a cultural insider with a taste for in-jokes-within-in-jokes:

Sir, – Last week Mrs Hugh Daubeny failed to provide a correct solution to the Crossword puzzle, and I feel this is worthy of notice in your correspondence columns.

> Dear Mrs Hugh Daubeny,
> What has occurred?
> I will not believe
> You were stumped
> For a word.
>
> ...
>
> Week after week
> – Nay, year after year
> To you is this
> Crossword still
> Perfectly clear.
> Then what freak of fortune
> Has dogged Mrs Hugh
> And led her at last
> To this grim Waterloo?

Sadly, however, after a row, which led to her leaving home, the silver spoon had been snatched from her mouth. Her father disowned her, forbidding communication with her mother, whilst her uncle, the 7th Duke, and the Wellesley family, kept her at arm's length. A paternal aunt made her a small allowance, which paid the rent on a spacious attic flat in Highgate, 'High over Archway', as Wright recalls it, but the early forties were years of extreme poverty. Orde had to balance her career against her responsibilities as a single parent and sole breadwinner. Her baby, Emily, was born in February 1943. The father, a refugee Polish pilot in the Canadian Air Force, had abandoned them by the summer of 1944. At the same time, Orde found herself at the heart of two of the most celebrated artistic communities of the age, the legendary Soho, 'when

Soho really was its legend' (Wright); and the briefer scene in Glasgow, inaugurated and sponsored by David Archer at the height of the Blitz. As revealed in a 'fascinating' forties diary (no longer extant), Orde's qualities both as a writer and as a mother are affirmed by Wright:

> I knew her so well & shared some of the experiences she writes about – & what a good mother she was … these pages show how broke poor Julian was and how well she looked after her baby & what sacrifices she made (all this without self-pity). The writing is excellent, J. had a fine eye for the comic & a sharp one for … characters & foibles.

Light verse apart, Orde's first recorded publication was in October 1943. 'Conversation', a story about a loner in the Blitz, appeared in the first number of *Writing Today*, edited by Peter Ratazzi and Denys Val Baker, two of the most active figures in the little magazine world. A consistent supporter of Orde's work, Baker contributes a story, 'The Horseman', to the third Apocalyptic anthology, *The Crown and the Sickle*, published by the same Staples Press in 1944.

'A Girlfriend of Graham's'

Archer left London for Glasgow early in 1941, opening another in a series of uncommercial bookshops as well as the Scott Street Arts Centre. He 'stimulated artistic life in Glasgow even though the Centre itself lasted only eighteen months' (Michael and Margaret Snow); and also provided free accommodation and studio space for artists in his flat in Sandyford Place, a handsome terrace in the West End. In 1941, whilst working at a torpedo factory on the Clyde,

Graham had been invited to move in by the painter (and later theosophist prophet) Benjamin Creme. Residents included the film-maker and sculptor Helen Biggar, who had collaborated on the experimental anti-war film, *Hell Unltd*, in 1936, and the artists, Robert Frame, Josef Herman and Jankel Adler. Both Poles had lost almost their entire families in the Holocaust. A veteran of the Polish Army (and of the Nazi exhibition of Degenerate Art), discharged with heart trouble after evacuation from Dunkirk, Adler influenced a generation of neo-romantic artists, including the Scottish couple, Robert Colquhoun and Robert MacBryde (already based in London, but often returning to Glasgow), John Minton, Michael Ayrton, Keith Vaughan and Prunella Clough. The younger of the two, Herman, had discovered Creme, and was later to mentor the Glasgow poet, Burns Singer, himself descended from Polish Jews, and soon, as a teenager, to become a 'fanatic disciple' of Graham.

It was in Glasgow that Graham and Julian Orde appear to have met, 'probably', says Wright, 'in David Archer's bookshop', where she may have been employed. Like all his ventures in this line, it had 'collapsed under the weight of its proprietor's immense open-handedness and absolute vagueness'. Orde's contributor's note to *Writing Today* mentions that she has written 'a number of sketches about Scottish life' (none preserved), which suggests that she may have spent some time in the city. From late 1941, Graham spent over a year working as a poet-in-residence (long before it was a thing) at Kilquhanity House, a progressive school in Galloway, run on the same principles as Summerhill, which had opened in 1940. Acting in repertory in the city in 1942, Orde was soon staying at Sandyford Place, now, according to the Snows, 'a girlfriend of Graham's'. There were complications, however, on both sides. Orde's affair with the father of her child must have begun by around May 1942, and she was probably back in London when she gave birth to her daughter, in February 1943. Meanwhile, at Kilquhanity, Graham had begun an affair with a colleague, Mary Harris, an Oxford First with aspirations as a writer, who happened to own two seaside caravans at Praa Sands, near Marazion in Cornwall.

Frame describes a series of '"happenings", as they might now be termed', organised by Graham at Sandyford Place, aiming 'to co-ordinate the visual arts with that of poetry', to which Orde may well have brought her own multi-media skill-set:

> An environment was improvised from piled-up chairs, screens from the Centre and lengths of painter's canvas stretched into corridors like a kind of maze. The lighting was entirely by candlelight. The reading was contemporary poetry, including some of Sydney's own. The members of the audience were conducted … to certain strategic points where a part of the reading took place … then … to another area of the maze.

David Gascoyne and Dylan Thomas were amongst those who stayed in Sandyford Place for a week or two, Gascoyne in October 1941 and Thomas in July 1942. Reporting Thomas's visit in a letter, Graham added that 'The Centre just doesn't exist anymore'. The bookshop had also closed by the end of 1942. Sandyford Place, however, continued to be an informal communal meeting-place for around another eighteen months, until the spring of 1944.

Whilst he was dividing his time between Galloway and Glasgow, Graham's poetry began to attract attention. Despite having 'had absolutely nothing published yet', after rejections by John Lehmann and others, he had, by June 1942, persuaded, or, according to Frame, 'bullied' Archer into reviving his illustrious imprint. Both Thomas and Gascoyne had been published by the prescient Archer's Parton Press in the mid-thirties, which had also published George Barker's *Thirty Preliminary Poems* in 1933, two years before T.S. Eliot took him on at Faber and Faber, as he took Graham in 1947, publishing *The White Threshold* in 1949. First publication of these four poets, Barker, Thomas, Gascoyne and Graham, would represent publishing genius if Archer had published fifty books, and forty-six had been duds. Graham had already completed *The Seven Journeys*, but chose to publish first a more recent collection entitled *Cage Without Grievance*, illustrated in the neo-romantic style of Adler by Frame and Creme. By the time it came out in the autumn, Graham had had his first poems accepted by Tambimuttu, duly appearing in *Poetry (London)* No. 7, in November 1942. One of the earliest responses to his poetry is a fan-letter by Julian Orde, printed in *Poetry (London)* No. 9 in May 1943:

> Dear Sir, – The October-November number of *Poetry (London)* is memorable to me for the beauty of Henry Moore's cover and the first printing of W.S. Graham's poems. If the *Third Journey* is one of a series I hope you will publish the others, and if there are any more sonnets as lovely as the *Fourth Sonnet*, I hope you will publish those too.

Graham and Mary Harris spent the summer of 1943 in 'The Wheelhouse', as he had christened her caravans. He stayed on, but she returned to Kilquhanity, pregnant with their daughter, Rosalind. They had agreed to separate and decided that Rosalind should be brought up by her mother in Scotland, where she was born in the spring of 1944. Allowed to stay in The Wheelhouse, Graham lived alone in Germoe in the autumn of 1943, before returning to Glasgow around January

1944. In the spring, Archer wound up his Glasgow operations, then also returned to London, accompanied by evacuees from Sandyford Place. No less than three, Graham, Frame and Creme, took up residence in Orde's large Highgate flat, with much coming and going throughout the summer between the studios of John Minton, Adler and 'the two Roberts', and between Soho and 'the seacoast of Bohemia'. David Wright recalls the occasion, in the Wheatsheaf, in May 1944, of his first meeting with the 'contingent of painters, poets and novelists' who had 'emigrated ... from Glasgow with Sydney Graham' and 'erupted into Soho':

> Colquhoun and MacBryde ...; gentle Robert Frame and nervous Benjamin Creme; the novelist Fred Urquhart; Sydney's then girlfriend, Julian Orde, with whom I felt an instant rapport; and lastly the ... neurotic, bespectacled David Archer, 'quivering like an aspirin tree', a *New Statesman* tucked under his withered arm. All these – who, though I did not realise it then, were to be my friends for life – I met on that one evening.

By mid-August 1944, Graham had again left for Praa Sands, shortly to be reunited with Nessie Dunsmuir. Her partner, a Czech pilot with the Canadian Airforce named František Koranda, such a 'hit with her folks', Graham told Minton, that 'even her mother thinks she should marry him', was shot down by a German fighter over the North Sea in October 1944, with the loss of all nine crew on their B-24 bomber. Graham and Dunsmuir lived in the caravans at Germoe for over two years, and in Mevagissey for almost another year, before once again, in the autumn of 1947, agreeing to go their separate ways.

In the meantime, Graham made frequent forays into Soho. In September 1945, Orde informs Wright that he had returned to Cornwall after 'a worse holiday than usual': 'he was very ill during the last few days and vomited blood. I hardly saw anything of him'. By November, a pattern had been set, as Wright reports: 'W.S. Graham is coming up to town, which means he will drink all his money, get ill, & then go back to Cornwall to recuperate. He's done so often before'. The products of this regime include ulcers and 'The Nightfishing', begun by 1948.

'I Fear the Young Dog has Sold Me a Pup'

As well as her first story, D.V. Baker published Orde's first poem, in the third number of one of his own little magazines, *Voices*, around the autumn of 1944, catching the eye of A.T. Tolley, who singles out, in a survey of WWII literary magazines, 'the individual and lively fantasy, "Superstition", by the almost forgotten Julian Orde'. Her earliest poetry was also praised by Walter de la Mare, as reported to Wright: 'I had a wonderful letter ... saying my poems had given him great joy ... and would I come and spend an evening with him at Twickenham?' (Princeton University Library holds six letters, 'with commentary on her poems', dated 1944–45). During the same period, Baker printed another short story in *Writing Today*; and Charles Wrey Gardiner, another contributor to *The Crown and the Sickle*, took the first of several poems for *Poetry Quarterly*. 'The Awaiting Adventure' by Orde and 'The Day and Night Craftsman' by Graham appear on facing pages of the summer 1945 number, together with 'The Bay' by Wright, as noted by Graham in a letter to his friend: 'all in the one number, you me and J'.

In May 1945, Graham had commended another poem to Wright: 'Julian's poem "The Upward Rain" is good I think. I hope Dylan helps her towards publication'. No doubt he had got it from Wright, along with news of her recent, promising encounter with Dylan Thomas, 'who is said', according to Paul

Ferris, 'to have spent 8 May', VE Day, in her company. In his memoir, *Half an Arch*, Jonathan Gathorne-Hardy, later a colleague in an advertising agency, reports Orde's own account of 'a brief affair with Dylan Thomas': 'She said that one morning she'd got up to buy them breakfast and asked him if he wanted anything. "Yes", said Dylan, "leave your breasts on the bed"'. A letter written around mid-May by Thomas in Newquay to Orde in London is consistent with this yarn, and also with high hopes of his assistance:

> I'll send away, at once, the poems you sent me, to the few editors I know: Herring first, then Cyril C., then Muir of Orion – though you probably know him as well as I do, then Quennell of Cornhill; and will let you know ... I liked all the poems, but am not going to say anything about them yet because I am down, down, down among the live men, drowned in writs, terrified of the past, the knock, the crunch on the gravel ... I missed you, in fact, in theory, in every way, dearly. Next time I'll see more of you, may I? Have you got any more that I am allowed to see? No laughing at you, now or ever ... Believe me, I will write soon, and tell you about the poems. Love, always, Dylan.

The non-fulfilment of any or all of these weaselly promises prompted a rueful response:

> Dear Dylan oh why did you
> Not ring me up?
> I fear the Young Dog
> Has sold me a pup.
>
> We will meet once a year when
> The Wheatsheaf is dry

And you'll tell me a story
And once more I'll buy.

My arches are fallen
My morals laid low
Forsaken by Dylan
– yours faithfully – JO

There were no poems by Orde in *Life and Letters, Horizon, Orion* or *The Cornhill*. In 1946, however, she published two more in *Poetry Quarterly*; another in *Voices*; 'The Upward Rain' in *New Road*, the Apocalyptic annual edited by Fred Marnau (who also contributed a story to *The Crown and the Sickle*); and 'The Changing Wind', in the Christmas number of the BBC weekly, *The Listener*. 'The Upward Rain' was commended in a waspish review of *New Road* in *The Windmill*, a miscellany edited by Kay Dick. In its entirety, the only review of Orde's poetry to appear in her lifetime reads as follows: 'there are good poems by David Wright, Julian Orde and Thomas Good'. The next year, Wrey Gardiner, whose Grey Walls Press published *New Road* as well as his magazine, printed more of Orde's poems in *Poetry Quarterly*, whilst her other most enthusiastic British editor, D.V. Baker, reprinted a poem, 'The Lovers', from his little magazine, *Voices*, in a handsome 350-page hardback anthology for the American publisher, Vanguard. *Modern British Writing* features prose by Kenneth Clark, George Orwell and Stephen Spender and poems by Dylan Thomas, R.S. Thomas, J.F. Hendry, Vernon Watkins, Graham, Denise Levertoff (as she was still spelling her name) and Lynette Roberts. Also in 1947, the enterprising editor of *The Windmill*, Kay Dick, alias Jeremy Scott, selected a story, 'The Florist', for *At Close of Eve: An Anthology of New Curious Stories*, alongside Frank Baker, William Sansom, James Hanley, Fred Urquhart and a brilliant group of women, including Ida Affleck-Graves, Phyllis Shand Allfrey, Elizabeth Berridge and Stevie Smith.

Amongst other readers to whom Orde's poems appealed was the American poet Kenneth Rexroth, who took 'The Changing Wind' from *The Listener* for his classic anthology, *The New British Poets*, published by James Laughlin's New Directions in 1949. It is probably also thanks to Rexroth – just possibly to Thomas! – that a superb set of seven had appeared, in 1948, in *New Directions in Prose and Poetry*, the 'annual exhibition of divergent literary trends' edited by Laughlin, alongside locals such as Tennessee Williams, Carson McCullers and the rising star, Richard Wilbur; a strong European contingent including Paul Eluard, Eugenio Montale and George Seferis; and a brace of Apocalyptics in Watkins and Alex Comfort.

By 1949, then, Julian Orde had published around a dozen poems, appeared in *The Listener*, and contributed to two prestigious American anthologies. This would seem to represent sustainable success, yet she never published another poem. Robin Skelton selected 'The Changing Wind' for the Penguin anthology, *Poetry of the Forties*, in 1968, but although she continued to write and submit poems, it was only after her death in 1974 that she began to receive her due. She may have had enough of a reputation as a forties poet to have been damned by association, but, other than that of her momentum until 1949 and subsequent disappearance, there is no evidence that this was so; and it is also possible that she wrote next to no poetry during the fifties. Only one poem is definitely assignable to the decade – at best, a fallow period.

'On the stage for six years', according to a 1948 contributor's note, Orde played a large variety of parts in the theatre and on the radio, including a role in *Jeannie* at Hull New Theatre in 1942, alongside the young Paul Scofield, later to win an Oscar for his portrayal of Sir Thomas More in *A Man for all Seasons*. Premiered in 1936, filmed in 1941, televised in 1946, and revived in 2018, *Jeannie*, by Aimée Stuart, follows the fortunes of a young Glaswegian woman freed from drudgery by the death of her father, as she squanders her inheritance before finding true love.

Orde's credits include a run as leading lady with the Harrogate Repertory Company in 1945, but by this date the emphasis had shifted to the BBC, as she took part in over twenty radio shows, beginning with 'Children's Hour' in May 1944. She progressed to productions by the renowned Douglas Cleverdon, such as 'A Parsonage in the Hesperides', a portrait of Robert Herrick, in September 1944. In 1946, she played Celia in a Shakespeare spin-off, 'Touchstone and Audrey', and took the role of Alice, the French barmaid, alongside Dylan Thomas as Private Dai Evans, in Cleverdon's radio production of *In Parenthesis* by David Jones (and the same role, now joined by Richard Burton as Private Thomas, in the remake of November 1948). That summer, she reprised the role of Bessie for the TV production of *Jeannie*, starring Barbara Mullen (Janet in *Doctor Finlay's Casebook*) and John Laurie, later famous as Private ('We're all doomed!') Fraser in *Dad's Army*, with whom Orde had a brief affair, perhaps shortened by his refusal to spend four-and-six on a packet of Russian cigarettes (see 'Fond Rebuke for a Grudged Gift').

Her acting and writing careers converged when she began working for Concord Productions, a commercial film producer with a government contract, around 1944. Working from Old Compton Street in Soho, Orde wrote the scenarios for training films for the Services, such as *Driving Instruction*, for RAF vehicle drivers, enlivening the Highway Code with staged minor incidents, and *Naval Demolitions*, a manual of methods of detonation. Her talent for surreal comedy found an outlet in a series of Pythonesque skits on her employers:

> In a crowded railway carriage a man called Basil opened … his suitcase and took out a small cardboard box. After replacing the case in the rack he made his way to the window and scattered white powder along the line. With an air of relief he sat down.
>
> The man opposite could not resist asking: 'Why did you do that?'
>
> Basil leaned forward. 'Just clearing the track of elephants old boy,' he said, 'That stuff's fatal to 'em, absolutely fatal.'
>
> 'But there are no elephants in England,' exclaimed the man opposite.
>
> Craftily, Basil whispered: 'I know. But that wasn't the real powder!'
>
> At this point an adjacent straphanger rapped out: 'You haven't mentioned Concord Productions Ltd – this is supposed to be an advertisement you know.'

Around 1945, a letter to Wright portrays a confident, resourceful and gifted woman, poised between poverty and affluence, with insider-status, tantalisingly, just out of reach:

> A friend in the Scenario Institute got me outside film reading to do – bringing in about three guineas a week.

Donald Taylor – my film boss – wrote that he cannot offer me a contract and there just isn't any freelance work at the moment, but he recommended me very highly to someone else who might want me permanently. I saw him yesterday – not such a charming or amusing or cultivated outfit as Donald's and Dylan's, but nice, and doing the same sort of stuff. He said he is definitely looking for writers and asked how much money I would expect on a permanent contract? I looked out of the window, pressed my sweaty hands together, ... and trying to keep my voice normal, said A Thousand a Year. 'Well, that's not unreasonable' he answered. He said they could not take anyone permanently just yet, but he had some freelance work ... and would send it within the next fortnight. He asked what Donald paid me ... said he would pay me half as much again. So things are looking brighter. It seems a good moment to get in on this outfit, they are still starting and have not enough writers or film directors or anyone ... What is annoying is that I owe money to everyone ..., and I have to rob Peter to pay Paul all the time, but still, when the freelance work comes maybe I'll be able to manage.

With his partner John Grierson, renowned for his documentaries at the GPO Film Unit, Donald Taylor was the 'boss' at the famous Strand Films in Soho Square. His inspired recruitment of Dylan Thomas resulted in a series of films for the Ministry of Information, which, according to Conservative politician Lord Boothby, 'did not win the war, but ... certainly won the election for Labour'. The Scenario Institute, a prestigious project of huge ambition, was conceived as a British Hollywood Academy by Filippo del Giudice, impresario and crony of Ernest Bevin and Sir

Stafford Cripps. Sponsored by J. Arthur Rank, it was scuttled by the screenwriters' union, whose fears of monopoly were misplaced, for what del Giudice had in mind was to attract 'the literary talent of the industry', including Rebecca West and Compton Mackenzie, to 'a University of the Motion Picture'. Orde may have done similar 'freelance work' on the filmic potential of new novels for Paramount Productions, the British wing of the Hollywood corporation, since there is a draft of a poem on one of their synopsis-proformas, but the start-up to which she refers must be yet another 'outfit'. At this point, then, she had excellent contacts and irons in the fire, but little reliable income to show for it all. At the end of 1945, she moved two miles north to a smaller flat at No. 22 Muswell Hill, presumably to economise.

'Melodrama as English and as Excellent as Muffins'

By 1947, however, she had landed her lucrative job, with the leading advertisers, S.H. Benson, in Kingsway Hall, Holborn. The firm specialised in large poster campaigns for accounts such as Rowntree's chocolate, Colman's mustard and Guinness, with 'Guinness is good for you!' amongst its hit slogans, but also produced film advertisements, for which, as she explains to Wright in a letter on 3 February, Orde had overall responsibility: 'I write the scripts of ad. films, & run all the money side, policy & distribution as well. I have secretary & 2 assistants. God knows whether I will be able to keep it up – it's very difficult. (£700 a year)' (add two noughts for the approximate equivalent salary in 2024). She was well able to do so, as it turned out, and when S.H. Benson became Ogilvy & Mather, she continued in the same line of work.

Her involvement with this branch of the film industry had led within two years to one of Orde's greatest professional successes, a joint credit for the screenplay of a BAFTA-nominated feature film. In 1943, Anthony Havelock-Allan and Ronald Neame had formed Cineguild with David Lean, under the aegis of J. Arthur Rank, making *Brief Encounter* with Noel Coward in 1945; in 1947, however, the pair broke away to form their own short-lived outfit, Constellation Films. In 1948, they made *The Small Voice*, based on the novel by Robert Westerby, directed by Fergus McDonell (Oscar-nominated for the Belfast thriller, *Odd Man Out*, in 1947) and co-written by Neame, George Barraud, a silent screen actor, and Julian Orde. It gave Howard Keel his film debut, after starring on Broadway in *Oklahoma* (later in *Annie Get Your Gun*, 1950; and the TV super-soap, *Dallas*, in the 1980s), as an escaped convict, with Valerie Hobson (title role, *Bride of Frankenstein*, opposite Boris Karloff, 1935; Estella in *Great Expectations*, 1946) as a virtuous hostage. In the *Spectator*, Virginia Graham commended a 'melodrama as English and as excellent as muffins', but relieved by acerbic wit, as when the children start correcting the villain on his grammar, perhaps attributable to (and inherited by) Orde. In a scintillating polemic in *Sequence*, the influential film magazine edited by the young Lindsay Anderson, *The Small Voice* is contrasted with 'recent British features' which offer 'nothing worth even adverse criticism' and credited with no less than redeeming the 'prestige' of the British film industry:

> [T]he poor output of today is getting by ... on the prestige earned by films of the War period and the first year or so of peace. And ... the fallacy has come to be ... accepted that 'prestige' (i.e. good) pictures must cost, and lose, millions. That this is not so is proved by *The Small Voice*, ... a British melodrama which avoids ... the usual pitfalls. There is no overplaying of minor parts, no cockney or regional 'humour', no slushy

background music ... [but] excitement, atmosphere, interesting characterisation and ... craftsmanship ... [T]he screenplay ... by Derek Neame and Julian Orde is well written, with good dialogue and no time wasted; the acting is of a high standard, particularly by ... Keel as the leader of the convicts ... Camerawork ... and editing are both admirable.

In August 1949, Orde married Ralph Abercrombie, a fellow-copywriter, son of the Georgian poet, Lascelles Abercrombie, 'and one of the better critical intellects of our time, though an inhibiting modesty prevented him from harvesting his exceptional talents' (Wright):

Apart from a few reviews, some exquisite letters and the memory of his talk, he left nothing behind to show what he was, or might have done. They were well-suited – ideally, I thought ... Now that she was respectable, Julian's father and aristocratic relations rallied round – there were invitations to Strathfieldsaye and so forth.

Orde continued to take part in radio productions, such as *The Face of Violence*, a 'symbolical portrait of the manifestations and motives of violence in modern society' by Jacob Bronowski, produced by Cleverdon, in March 1950, playing one of the Heavenly Twins; *I Know My Way* by Joyce Rowe, produced by D.G. Bridson in May 1951, in which four characters reminisce about a prospective nun, before coming to terms with her choice; and a remake of *Pytheas*, an ambitious verse play by Henry Reed about the ancient Greek explorer of Britain, in June 1952.

In March 1950, she took pride of place, opposite Dylan Thomas, in a spread in *Picture Post*. In the most avant-garde feature ever to grace its pages, on a read-through of Picasso's play, 'Desire Caught by the Tail', at the ICA, Orde is shown, in patrician profile, abusing Reggie Smith (Guy Pringle in the *Fortunes of War* novels by his wife Olivia Manning). 'Thin Anxiety' has choice lines to contend with, as she helps herself to the sturgeon: 'the bitter erotic flavour of these delicacies keeps my depraved taste for spiced and raw dishes panting eagerly'.

By this time, the couple had moved two miles south, back down Muswell Hill Road, to The Park, Highgate, where they were still living in 1955, and may have spent the rest of the fifties and the early sixties, before moving west, right across Hampstead, to Lyndale Avenue, in Child's Hill, by the beginning of 1963.

In October 1952, Lady Eileen died. In 1968, Orde recalls the 'aftermath' in a letter to Wright:

> I never got over the shock of the aftermath of my mother's death, when my father, uninterested in the past, made Ralph and my sister and me put practically all papers onto a bonfire burning merrily in the garden. Although we each stole quite a lot, in the end, through sheer fatigue, we obeyed him, and history and capital were burnt.

'I Imagine that More Will Be Heard of Her'

Professional involvement paid dividends once again in 1953, with BBC Third Programme productions of two plays of her own, and an auspicious *Radio Times* write-up in December:

> For an original radio play that is distinctly original, I venture to commend Julian Orde's *The Dentist on the Dyke* ... [I]n ability to cope with the ridiculous,

and to sit on the fence between the pathetic and the comic, this is rather Chekhovian ... [I]n its touches of macabre humour, and creation of a private world of sinister fun, it puts one in mind of an Addams cartoon ... a mixture of the sly, the absurd, the subtle, and very funny ... [Her] previous radio play, My *Landlord is a Rat*, attracted some attention in the summer, and I imagine that more will be heard of her ... [T]he dominant character is a formidable dentist named Mr de Hoot, who does not appear; we see the effects of his personality on his wife and on Mr Lott, a mild, little man of fifty who is booking clerk at the local Variety palace. They both hate and fear Mr de Hoot, and ... conspire to be rid of him.

The reviewer in *The Listener* was a little sharper, but also found promise in the playwright:

This adventure in the farcical-macabre-pathetic got us nowhere in particular. Still, its author, Julian Orde, has a sense of fantasy that we can expect to blossom. His [sic] gift is for the grave presentation of the wilder humours [in] a town that appeared to depend for entertainment upon ... town hall lectures on 'The Teeth of Aboriginal Peoples'.

For all the success of Orde's emergence as a playwright, there were no more plays; and after several radio roles in the early fifties, these, too, peter out, with only one more appearance, in the 1955 remake of *In Parenthesis* (Burton now taking the lead as John Ball and the voice of Dylan Thomas as Dai Evans 'interpolated' into the transmission). Meanwhile, her advertising career went from strength to strength, which may go far towards an explanation. During the fifties she was gathering a reputation as one of the brightest stars of her profession.

If Orde had, as Wright recalls, 'stopped showing me ... poems', she continued to respond generously to his, in particular, in March 1954, to his sequence, 'A Voyage to Africa', 'your best and most satisfying poem': 'I think it's extraordinary to have your longest poem your best' (a compliment precisely returned by Wright, when he came across 'Conjurors' after her death).

Ralph Abercrombie had been associated with David Archer since the thirties, and when, in 1956, in Greek Street, Soho, Archer opened the last of a series of munificent but commercially ill-fated bookshops, Abercrombie undertook to manage it, as recalled by the poet Dom Moraes:

> In the back half was a small but excellent lending library, consisting mostly of rare books, and a coffee bar. Archer planned to start a gallery in the basement, also part of the shop. He showed us round with a prim nervous smile, and frequently apologised for the fact that he was not yet doing a roaring trade ... Abercrombie, a kind, dryly witty man, watched Archer as a trainer might watch an unreliable animal.

As he had in Glasgow in the forties, Archer succeeded in recreating the ambience of his Parton Street bookshop in Holborn in the thirties, which appears to have been his sole aim:

> Archer's shop had reached its ... high summer. It was now always full, but unfortunately not of customers. Every young writer in town used it as a club, drank free coffee there and borrowed the books ... Because of this constant clutter of writers, the shop took on the air of a *kibbutz*: everyone ... volunteered for work, and, under Ralph Abercrombie's austere

direction, shifted shelves, counted stock, or served
… Customers, looking in and finding the place filled
with eccentric young men who … all talked loudly
to each other … and dropped ash everywhere, would
depart hastily. Those who did [not] found it difficult
to buy anything. Archer had an aristocratic prejudice
against taking money [and] either recommended
them to another bookshop … or gave them books
free … Abercrombie stopped this …, but since he
wasn't always there, the turnover was … low.

The shop may not have shown a profit, but there were
unforgettable moments:

Archer mounted an exhibition of mobiles in the
gallery. The largest one, which hung from the ceiling,
was a kind of iron windmill. The night before the
opening, David Wright, Ralph Abercrombie and
I went down to inspect it. 'Does it move?' inquired
Wright, and pulled at one of the flanges. Not only
did the windmill move, it spun round fiercely, and
caught Ralph a sharp crack on the head, knocking
him unconscious.

In January 1957, Wright reports that 'Abercrombie has finally
left Archer's bookshop': 'Archer was literally driving him to
drink with his hysteria and indecision'. Within months, it had
closed, and by 1959, Archer was destitute, rescued only by a
Trust Fund organised by Wright.

Wright, who repeatedly tried to tempt him into contributing
to *Nimbus*, to no avail, 'had more respect for Ralph Abercrombie
than anybody I have known, both as a person & for his literary
knowledge & discrimination'. A shrewd reviewer, Abercrombie

had, in 1940, dismissed *The New Apocalypse* in *Time & Tide* as 'not a very interesting volume', scoring a direct hit: 'it is full of bad (or rather good) imitations of Dylan Thomas'. In the same review, he finds George Barker's poetry 'often moving', with its 'apocalyptic Blakean revolutionary attitude', despite faults so obvious as to constitute 'a permanent defect in the writer's talent – or genius'; and shows well-informed discrimination in excepting 'earlier poems' by Glyn Jones from his strictures: 'he, like Mr Treece and the other horsemen of the Apocalypse, has been dangerously fascinated by Mr Dylan Thomas's work'. He 'particularly' commends the marvellous 'Esyllt', written in 1933, the year before Jones's first, initially almost overwhelming, encounter with Thomas's poetry. As an acknowledged influence on the taste of Wright, the finest anthologist of the mid-century, Abercrombie thus combined admiration for the 'apocalyptic' quality of the major poets of the forties with disdain for the Apocalyptic movement, a distinction later explicitly formulated by Wright, with ironic consequences for his valuation, during her lifetime, of Julian Orde's poetry. By the mid-fifties, however, according to Abercrombie himself, 'his stock ... as a reviewer' was 'rock-bottom', perhaps because his taste had ossified. In a letter to Wright in April 1955, he declines a commission to review Marianne Moore:

> I don't know her stuff as well as I ought: I respect her and think she's really good sometimes; but always have some reservations, prejudiced ones, no doubt. The fact is, I think the old lady's a bit too <u>modern</u> for me – too avant-garde – and too un-English for the roots of my appreciation are really au fond very English. I am getting near a favourite subject of mine ..., and she'd be a good starting-point – but it would take too long ... [A]nyhow the main thing is I wouldn't do her ... justice ... Now Julian has a real

feeling for her, but of course hates the idea of writing anything approaching 'criticism'.

Self-parodic in its dry humour ('au fond very English'), this is the voice of a superannuated Georgian (no disrespect to Abercrombie senior), all too cosy with his prejudices. Dispiritingly, his hobby-horse seems to be a chauvinistic anti-modernism in harmony with the Movement against which Wright was already conducting a resolute editorial campaign, sketched out for his parents in February 1956, when *Time & Tide* had just recruited his ally Anthony Cronin:

> There is a literary war going on – read Cronin's article in *Nimbus* about Wain & Amis – These people have got hold of the *Spectator*, the *Twentieth Century*, [with] a foothold in the *London Magazine*; well, now we've got *Nimbus*, *Time & Tide*, and *Encounter*!

'He Was (A) Tight (B) Not Reading His Stuff But Singing It in a Thick Irish Accent'

One memorable occasion, on 17 November 1961, the disastrous last of a series of poetry readings which, improbably, Wright had been invited to organise on behalf of the John Lewis department store, begins with scapegrace Brian Higgins ('that bloody menace, a pure poet') on his best behaviour and ends with dinner chez Abercrombie in the company of Stevie Smith:

> This time I asked Brian Higgins to compere the reading, and he did it well, the fiasco wasn't his fault … We kicked off with Stevie Smith who is always good, & followed her with Kavanagh. This was where

the thing got wrecked ... Kavanagh ... was waving his arms around & rocking about in rumbustious fashion, then I saw that the audience was getting pretty restless & after a bit one or two got up & slipped out. Then Kavanagh ran over his time & when poor Higgins tried to get him off the platform he was waved off ... [H]e seemed set to go on all night, but after 15 minutes he paused for a moment so I [gave] the signal for the interval ... I took the opportunity to ask Julian Abercrombie how Kavanagh was reading & she told me he was (a) tight (b) not reading his stuff but singing it in a thick Irish accent and said no one could understand a word. So I told Higgins to ... call Stevie, but omit the second dose of Kavanagh ... [A]s a matter of fact the John Lewis bloke gave [him] no chance ... because when Stevie finished her second stint he got up & firmly closed the reading. Kavanagh was black with fury & roared up & down the room claiming he'd been insulted. Anyway, I'd had enough & as Julian had a car slipped out with her & Stevie & left them to sort it out among themselves ... Julian took us to her home off the Finchley Road & we all had dinner with her & Ralph.

No longer an outsider or a maverick, Wright was now at the height of his authority, a respected poet and curator of contemporary poetry as the editor of influential anthologies and two widely-admired magazines, *Nimbus*, in the mid-fifties, and *X: A Quarterly Review*, co-edited with the Irish painter Patrick Swift from 1959 to 1962. *Nimbus* had printed Kavanagh and Smith when no one else would, and both were appearing in the thriving *X*, but neither features Julian Orde.

In another letter to his mother, Wright records a visit to the Abercrombies in July 1963:

They were out, only the daughter, Emily, now aged 20, was in. She gave me some gin & we talked for about an hour in the garden (a very pretty one now). She told me that Ralph has had some sort of breakdown, & lives at a mental home, coming home for the weekends. She said he had lost all contact with reality. Also it turns out that Emily does not live with her mother, preferring to be independent – she lives in a bedsitter in the Caledonian Road & works as a waitress! … She told me that Ralph would be coming home at 6.30 & would want to see me … I had a drink in a pub then called … again … We sat in the garden & I must say I saw no sign whatever of any mental disturbance, on the contrary we had an extremely good conversation – he has a wonderful brain & great knowledge of poetry. Then Julian arrived & made us some supper. She is now an extremely successful businesswoman & has just had a play on the television which I gather did very well indeed. But there seemed signs of strain between her and Ralph, I may have been mistaken, and I hope I am, but she seemed rather impatient with him. Perhaps she feels he is useless. I hope I am wrong about this because I get fonder of Ralph every time I see him, one of the nicest & gentlest of men I have ever met.

An untitled draft depicts the same man, who 'lived' rather than 'wrote' poetry:

> Now I can love you again, now we are parting,
> My Siamese twin, my old, mad, faery father:
> My essence of all the good in all the men
> Who lived or wrote poetry; my strange and darling
> husband.

My opponent, friction, the enemy in my house:
The crying inside the walls, the only one
I could never influence: who strolled in, who influenced me,
Who struck and stuck to me – the astonished host.

Now you are going as lightly as you came
Your cardboard suitcases tied up with string
Years and years of me in them; yet they contain
No more than they brought, in 1949.

This is clearly a conflicted poem. It would be hard to reconcile the hyperbolical 'essence of all the good in all the men / Who lived or wrote poetry' with the 'the enemy in my house'.

In default of any sequel to Orde's successful radio play, *The Dentist on the Dyke* itself made a triumphant comeback. Renamed *The Lady and the Clerk*, it was televised in the summer of 1963 in the *Drama '63* series on ATV. Produced by Royston Morley, who had worked on BBC scripts with Dylan Thomas during the Blitz, it gave Olivia Hussey, who played the heroine in the Zeffirelli film of *Romeo and Juliet* in 1968, her 'first paying job' at the age of twelve. Orde's episode in this popular series was featured in the regular 'Play Bill' slot in *TV Times*:

> This is Julian Orde's first play for television – and in spite of the name, Julian is a woman. 'I find a man's name useful as a writer', she told me ... In the play, Mrs de Hoot (Christine Finn), in her later thirties, is separated from her husband, a dentist in a seaside town, [and] forced to resort to dressmaking to make ends meet. [S]he meets Mr Lott (George Benson), a man who admires her husband and at the same time desires [her]. Their developing friendship leads them to think of ways of ridding themselves of Mr de Hoot ... Christine Finn said, 'Julian Orde has written excellent dialogue for my part. Mrs de Hoot lives in a world of lies, and Mr Lott joins her in that dream world'.

'Many Admirable Examples of Women,
Such as Julian Orde Abercrombie'

Equally impressed, a colleague at *Advertisers Weekly* imagines an amusing scenario:

> Julian Orde, a creative plans executive of Mather & Crowther Ltd., made her television debut [in] *Drama '63* on Sunday night, [with] her comedy-thriller *The Lady and the Clerk* ... Monday's *Daily Telegraph* headlined its review 'Good acting in talented play' ..., while the *Times* spoke of 'the ... precision with which [she] conjured up her characters'. Watching her own play, Julian quite possibly saw some more of her work in the commercial break too – for she has written many TV films for Mather's clients.

Her 'lively agency' in the sixties is recalled by David Holmes: 'A lot of experimentation took place and I learnt a lot there from some heavyweight writers; Fay Weldon, Mary Gowing, Maurice Smelt and the pipe smoking Julian Orde'. Weldon is almost as famous for the slogan, 'Go to work on an egg!', as for her novels; and Gathorne-Hardy recalls a colleague's response to Gowing's rival genius-wheeze about a hen that crows when she's laid her egg, 'Because an egg is something to crow *about*!': 'Good, Mary, er, very good, yes, but, er, doesn't only the cock crow?' 'Well, *thank* you, Alec, that's a whole weekend's work down the drain!'

An online reviewer of a biography of Assia Wevill, an ex-colleague at the same agency, where 'results mattered and not gender', includes Orde's name in another respectful round-up:

> [C]opywriters at Ogilvy and Mather included many admirable ... women, such as Julian Orde

Abercrombie, the playwright, Fay Weldon, the novelist, Patricia Miller, a leading journalist, and the brilliant Anne Semple, [who] might well have invited chauvinist opprobrium for their ... proto-feminism. As males we respected them unconditionally.

Gathorne-Hardy received a Copywriting Award in 1964, judged by a panel which included his immediate superior, Orde. Nothing dodgy about this, incidentally: 'Judges do not rule on copy emanating from their own agencies'. I wish I felt as confident about *Half an Arch*:

> Julian Orde, with her man's name and clay pipe, was my group head and also had writing ambitions. While I was there she had a [TV] play accepted about a dentist ... Her marriage to an Abercrombie was rocky and she had intense, platonic, affair-like relationships with her young male copywriters ... [taking] us (usually singly) to the Wig and Pen Club in Fleet Street [to] get drunk ... She had had years of psychoanalysis and was in some ways difficult, but I grew fond of her. She was also complicated. She liked to dominate and could take offence. Sometimes she irritated me ... Although her ... companions were almost invariably male and despite, she said, her long almost sexless marriage, she never made passes at them. Yet she did at Anne Semple, so that pretty Canadian copywriter told me. Perhaps Julian really preferred women. Her attitude to advertising seemed ambivalent. As we drank we would giggle at its absurdity.

'Two Elements' is the finest of a number of poems that may be interpreted, on the assumption that the speaker is also female, as arising out of a love affair with a woman:

She's fine, albeit guarded
Whose dainty fingers trimmed my incandescence
To a drawing-room flame, then disregarded
What I could ill afford; this evanescence

Into something oozier, ill-thought-of,
For I leave too many traces.
I was gauche; I couldn't prove
The fineness of my flame against her graces.

Now she flames in beautiful mistrust
(My name is mud) pretending not to see me.
Should I extend a hand though crack and crust?
We were elemented differently.

In the January 1968 number of *Advertisers Weekly*, for which
Orde may well have developed a soft spot, 'the latest of the
Schweppes "prestige" ads' is given 'a round of applause':

> It has a fine picture of a twist of lemon angling into
> the bubble and uprush of tonic swooshed into a glass
> … To do justice to it … calls for the convoluted
> talents of [a] Gerard Manley Hopkins … But Miss
> Julian Orde, of Mather's, has a splendid stab at it:

> > A twist of lemon and the Tonic's bloom
> > Expand the little glass into a room
> > Furnished with globes that whisper as they rise;
> > Look closer, till the Tonic magnifies
> > The room into the universe, and see
> > Oceans and suns and moons and nebulae.

'With justice', notes the critic, 'she is given credit in the ad':
'By Julian Orde who claimed to have found the Secret of *Schhh
… in a dream, which she later forgot'. To this day, it remains

highly unusual to name a copywriter. Her sophistication and wit ('The French are stealing the secret of *Schhh ... Vous-Savez-Qui!*') were clearly prized by all in the industry. She also worked tirelessly at a bewildering variety of avocations, enumerated in a letter to Wright in 1968:

> I work so hard, so long, and at so many things. My job mainly, but I've usually several freelance things on – jobs for *Which?* magazine, ranging from testing to being on panels, or reviewing; marking exam papers; the odd painting commission; and recently I've become very involved with Art Schools and students, and sit on Committees, and have even undertaken to organise advertising courses and projects which may lead me to have to be a visiting lecturer at Art Colleges all over England.

It was in this capacity that Orde found herself at the epicentre of 'May 1968':

> I met the most militant element of Hornsey Art School, along with colleagues of mine, and soon realised that I was the only real sympathiser. I've also had discussions with Ealing Students and various Principals, and am still baffled to find that I am the only grown-up who understands what the students are talking about. (I don't mean the only grown-up in England who understands, but in whatever galère I'm in.) I suppose this is partly because I've never stopped being secretly a rebel, and partly because I interview about five young people a day for jobs (in copywriting). I find it as easy to understand their point of view as for R.D. Laing to empathise with a Schizophrenic.

The ringleader of the notorious all-night protests and sit-ins at Hornsey, replicated nationwide, was Kim Howells (later a minister in Blair's Labour government), whose supporters included sympathetic academics, at least one of whom was sacked. To the left of those of most of her acquaintance, Orde's politics might be inferred from 'Seminar at Brussels, January 1963', a bleak, Audenesque elegy for one of the twin exponents of the 'Butskellite' consensus, the leader of the Labour party, Hugh Gaitskell (the recipient of no other, as far as my reading goes).

'I was Very Bucked about My Poem in the Penguin'

In July 1968, Wright records another visit to London, 'saddened at the outset' by opening the *Times* 'to find myself reading the obituary ... of Ralph Abercrombie who had died a few days before':

> He and Julian Orde had been estranged, or were at least living separately, for the last few years; I knew he had been in & out of hospital a lot; he had become an alcoholic – though for myself I would never have suspected it. Drink did not kill him however, it was heart failure. The same morning I read the news I went to the French pub & there saw Julian Orde, very upset as you may imagine. I would have gone to the funeral, only there was no funeral; the Abercrombie family being atheists refused to have any kind of service at all ... He was only 53 and I really think one of the finest minds of his generation, though alas he could never be persuaded to write a book.

Living in Cumberland, by this date, Wright had been seeing rather less of Orde, visiting only 'about once every year or two', but her replies to his letters after her husband's death reveal the continuing depth of their friendship. On 15 December, she congratulates him on a recent talk in advance of the Penguin publication of *Deafness: A Personal Account* in 1969:

> It seems surprising that you were the first man to speak about deafness, in public, from experience – but the more marvellous that you did it. I have always thought you the undeafest deaf man I've ever met. I remember the first time we met – I didn't know you were deaf for an hour or two, and then only because someone (Sydney?) mentioned it to me. But I didn't mean just that, ... I mean the most un-cut-off, for one thing, and, for another, that you seem as aware of sound, of rhythm, and of common speech as any one – more so than most hearing people. I remember you once saying, of a word in a poem, '"Air" is such a <u>long</u> word ...' Of course you were right, but when I've quoted this hearing people, insensitive to pronunciation (if that's the right word) have said: 'Nonsense, it's only one syllable!' I don't understand how you <u>knew</u> it's a long word, because one dwells on the vowels, but you did ... But it's not just this interest in the sound of words, I think it's your colloquialness, your au-faitness with the latest jokes and phrases and words that makes it difficult to remember you're deaf.

Wright had lost his hearing due to scarlet fever when he was seven, so would have been able, to some extent, to remember pronunciation, but Orde's insight is nonetheless accurate. Their 'rapport' is such that she can share her pleasure in being anthologised in the Penguin *Poetry of the Forties*, with only the gentlest of rebukes to the anthologist who consistently left her out:

> I was very bucked about my poem in the Penguin. I wrote to Ralph ... and asked if he had engineered it, but he hadn't. (He was always cross with you for leaving me out of yours, and including Potts!) I've never met Skelton. I must congratulate him. It seems quite a good-value book for five bob, and has become my favourite Christmas present!

On 27 October, she had written to Wright about another anthology, the manuscript of her husband's own, which would naturally have included her, though it never saw the light of day:

> I suppose Ralph's anthology, plus the rough books, should be given to a Librarian to sort out and index ... I feel battered by the weight of books, letters, writings, drawings and paintings – and photographs. Nothing ever gets properly sorted and filed ... I stuff things into cellophane bags ..., and intend to deal with them better, later ... drawings by the Roberts, Jankel, Minton, a manuscript by Gascoyne, ... all now so precious.

By mid-December, she was near despair: 'I can see myself <u>not</u> doing anything ... just putting it off, thinking I will have time sometime, when I clearly do not'; yet finding it 'intensely moving': 'The effect of the handwriting, and the choice, is as though he had written them all'.

On 19 December, only four days after she had written to Wright, Orde's father died at Durham Place. In stark contrast to this letter, which teems with contingency and commitment, her elegy for both parents, entitled 'Uninteresting Sonnet', recalling how her father was so 'uninterested in the past' as to wish to destroy all trace of it, has been leached of all colour and emotion.

Her latest piece of writing to have come to light is her 'Letter to Pamela Vandyke Price', a satirical response to the cookery correspondent of *The Spectator*, which appeared in July 1972. Orde relates 'a recurring day-nightmare' in which a friend gives her a ring:

> 'Hallo Julian, I'm bringing Elizabeth David round to lunch with you today, if that's all right. I know how much you admire her, and we happen to be quite near you'.
>
> 'Oh my God'.
>
> 'Look Julian, Elizabeth is perfectly aware how frightened people are of entertaining her. But she really means it when she says she likes the simplest possible food'.
>
> 'Like what?'
>
> 'Well, for instance, any piece of pâté maison that you happen to have in your fridge. The coarser the better'.
>
> 'Oh'.
>
> 'Then a completely plain, very light soufflée. That would be all really. Perhaps a few of those little Greek olives, any good cheese, and freshly ground coffee'.
>
> 'What about wine?'
>
> 'Oh just the local wine'.
>
> 'We don't have local wine in Cricklewood' ...

Two years later, in August 1974, Wright has another shock to report:

> I am much upset by the news of Julian Abercrombie's sudden death which came over the telephone from her daughter Emily last night. We saw her only five weeks or so ago, when we called at her house ... & she was looking quite beautiful & well & happy. Bruce Bernard did tell me, ... about a fortnight ago ..., that Julian was worried by some symptoms; however, as I had seen her looking so well so recently, I didn't take it seriously. Apparently she went to hospital only a short while ago & they made an exploratory operation & found the trouble – cancer I believe – so advanced as to be almost inoperable. She chose not to be operated on, which is like her; & they put her on heroin so there was no pain, and she died quite soon. You will surely remember her & Ralph Abercrombie (who would have thought she would not survive him by 5 years?) I feel a great loss, 30 years' friendship and all that web of association & memories & common friendships suddenly broken. Also realise what a remarkable woman she was – almost nothing she couldn't do, and do well, write, paint, photograph, act, &c.

Gathorne-Hardy's recollections end on a different note, acknowledging the other side of Orde's ambivalence: 'Yet she was in fact passionate about her job, fanatical, and when, about fifteen years after I'd arrived, she was sacked in the most brutal manner, she soon got cancer and died'. In 'A Note on Julian Orde Abercrombie', published with fifteen of her poems in *PN Review* in 1978, Wright recalls their last meeting, 'one summer evening in 1974':

[M]y wife and I, *en route* for Cumberland, escaped the afternoon traffic-crawl up the Finchley Road by paying an unexpected call on Julian at her home in Lyndale Avenue. We had never seen her look so beautiful. Three weeks later she was dead ...

'The Julian Orde Summer'

As christened by W.S. Graham, in a poem for Wright's sixtieth, 'The Julian Orde Summer', the season of the onslaught of the doodlebugs, was an epoch in the lives of all Londoners. With a wave of civilian deaths in terrifying attacks, as fighting in France intensified following the D-Day landings, 'the summer of 1944', according to the historian Daniel Todman, 'was the most total moment of Britain's total war'. Two July letters from Julian Orde to David Wright are amongst the most extraordinary documents of this 'moment' ever to have come to light. On 8 July, Orde finds herself not only at the epicentre of the 'invisible battle' which, according to Churchill's speech to the House of Commons on the 6 July 'has now flashed into the open', as what she calls a 'P. Bomb', or Pilotless Bomb, wrecks a building and injures friends as near as the next street, but also, with half of Soho coming and going and a clash at the Poetry Society about 'the Apocalyptic school', at the intersection of several artistic and literary circles:

> Dear David, It is in the evening: I am in bed ... Sydney is having a drink with Peggy Jean at the Wheatsheaf ... The sirens have gone but there is quietness. (And now not any more: a bumbling P. Bomb is about, somewhere.) ... Maurice Lindsay has organised a poetry evening at which Sydney & I have each been asked to read poems. It is on Friday at, I think 5. At

first I said no, because of the almost-decided weekend at your mama's, then I thought it would be a Good Thing to meet Lindsay & the poetry blokes, so I have said yes, if I can get Emily looked after at that time: at this moment I cannot think of any one able to look after her, so nothing is settled. Until about 3 days ago I was not especially nervous at the raids, & slept well all nights but one: then together came Churchill's speech, the ceiling falling and Beni's constant tension and jumpiness and near-panic, ... and all this has made me very worried at the P. Bombs ... A lot of bombs this morning: one came on a long glide, beginning by being just a buzzer in the far off distance & stopping so we thought it wd land on Kensington, & then gliding half across London towards us till its glide got very loud & we dashed downstairs. It exploded a street away on a tenement. More of our ceiling came in and my great Highgate friends, Mary & Cecil Stewart rang up to say their flat was quite wrecked & they both cut. We started to go round to them, all the streets full of glass & cut people & ambulances, but Mary came running out with blood on her to say not to come, no place for babies and other friends were there helping. So we came back, & here we are, the bombs still coming, and us all a bit shaken ... This letter has been thrice interrupted by the scramblings of Beni & me down the stairs, into Emily's room, and then rather sheepishly, up the stairs, back to our posts, I in my bed with the inkpot on the wireless, Beni reading my new copy of 'Scottish Art & Letters'. (Not a very good 5/- worth ... nothing very exciting ... save a poem by Sydney, almost his best, that ends: –

'... no, I'll inherit
No keening in my mountainhead or sea,
Nor fret for few who die before I do'.

These lines ... have a profound braveness I think
and are incidentally an important part of Sydney's
philosophy.) David Archer & my pen-pal Chuck &
Sydney & Beni have been here today, what a lot of
people ... Sydney has just come in, very tight.

Continuous with the courage of Londoners throughout the
war and equally with the 'philosophy' of Graham's poetry, this
letter is a unique record of the impact of Churchill's speech,
two days earlier, explaining why his Government had disclosed
no previous information, then proceeding to give, in his own
phrase, a 'brutally frank' account:

[W]e had by July, 1943, succeeded in locating at
Peenemunde, on the Baltic, the main experimental
station both for the flying bomb and the long-range
rocket. In August last the full strength of Bomber
Command was sent out to attack those installations
... Under the pressure of our counter-measures, the
enemy developed ... prefabricated structures which
could be rapidly assembled and well camouflaged,
especially during ... cloudy weather ... As new sites
are constructed or existing ones repaired, our bombing
attacks are repeated ... This invisible battle has now
flashed into the open ... This form of attack is ... of
a trying character ... but people have just got to get
used to that ... [F]lying bombs ... have killed almost
exactly one person per bomb ... 2,754 ... launched ...
2,752 fatal casualties sustained ... [L]et me say that
the casualty and first-aid services of Greater London

are ... not at all strained ... beyond [their] capacity ... [W]e prepared for so many more casualties in the Battle of Normandy than have ... occurred so far that we have, for the present, a considerable immediate emergency reserve ... I am glad to say that penicillin, ... up to now ... restricted to military uses, will be available for the treatment of all flying bomb casualties ... It may be a comfort to some to feel that they are sharing in no small degree the perils of our soldiers overseas and that the blows which fall on them diminish those which ... would have smitten our fighting men and their Allies.

It was no 'comfort' to Orde. In contrast, writing to his father at around the same date from his office at the *Sunday Times*, Wright echoes Churchill's sentiments, if not the speech itself:

[T]he buzz-bombs are busting the same as usual, but I feel quite indifferent to them in the daytime. It's another thing altogether in the small hours. I hope by the time this gets to you they'll be finished with. Anyway, it's rather nice to think we're taking some of the weight off the lads in Normandy by absorbing so much HE here in London.

Wright had earlier given a riveting account of the perils of both fronts. His friend, the dancer and choreographer Walter Gore, was later to be invalided out of the Navy, suffering from post-traumatic disorder: 'I was much shocked by the change in him, he looks worn out & doesn't seem interested in anything at all. It will be 6 months before he can dance again'. His role on D-Day had been to land infantry on the Normandy beaches from the vessels known as LCI (Landing Craft Infantry): 'the shore batteries didn't find their range until every man had been safely landed – not one casualty – but when his ship drew away they hit it & sank it and he was taken on another ship, which was also sunk'. But Wright was aware of none of all this in June, when he had stayed with Gore's wife:

> I was spending the night at Sally's flat in Knightsbridge, because she is so worried over her Wally … & hasn't heard from him since it started, which isn't very surprising, as he must be worked to death … [W]e'd just had supper when a terrific racket broke out, our old friends the rocket guns, & I dashed to the landing window … It was raining & there were … low clouds, & away in the direction of Chelsea a couple of searchlights, coned, were racing towards the flat. In a second I saw they were illuminating a plane – it looked like a fighter to me – flying very low and just tearing along. It went right over the flat chased by red Bofors tracers. I rushed to the other side of the house, another Bofors opened up, the plane was so low that the … shells looked as if they were going to chip off the chimney pots … The plane was still coned by the same searchlights, but they'd come to the end of their range, and the boys of Notting Hill were a bit slow on the uptake because they didn't pick it up with their lights. However the horizon suddenly filled with a big red splash, & that was the end of Jerry. Gosh, I felt sorry for the poor devil. He must have been scared stiff – I've never seen an aeroplane move so quickly. It was probably an illusion, but he seemed to be going faster than the Bofors tracers!

The reason for the astounding speed of the plane is that it wasn't a plane at all, but a doodlebug:

Yes, isn't that a pathetic description of the end of a pilotless plane on the first page of this letter! I didn't know what it was then, it didn't come out until the afternoon, in the evening papers. Since then life has been one long air raid. The damn things are always coming over. I never know when there's a raid on or not; but there are so many it doesn't matter. I was up Tottenham Court Road one day when one of them dropped south of Shaftesbury Avenue. I went there at once & watched them digging dead & wounded from the rubble (I wasn't allowed to help; there were plenty of experts & I think it must be a pretty specialised business.) It was a bad sight altogether.

During the crisis, Wright grew closer to both Orde and Graham, in whose absence, later in July, as well as staying over in Highgate, he arranged a visit to a friend, the poet Ida Affleck-Graves:

I am taking J & her baby down to Ida this week. Sydney has gone to Cornwall. (I'm hoping to spend my holiday with him either in Cornwall or walking in Scotland.) Julian needs a rest from these P-planes, she is absolutely whacked.

In a letter to his mother on 9 August, Wright records a close encounter: 'I saw another P-plane go over on Friday night I think when we were driven into the garden. It made a horrible noise and bust somewhere else'. This is the occasion recalled in his elegy, 'On a Friend Dying':

The summer of pilotless planes
Of searchlit nights and soft,
When once upon a scare

Together we ran out

Into the naked garden
High over Archway, and
The warm leaves of laurel
Trembled in no wind.

From unidentified flying objects to the 'flying bombs' of Churchill's official announcement, through the changing nomenclature of 'pilotless planes' and 'buzz-bombs' to resignation to the 'damn things ... always coming over', the social history of the V1 campaign is complete.

'As for these So-Called Poets of The New Apocalypse?'

The second of these letters, dated 15 July 1944, gives a priceless account of the event at the Poetry Society. In the foyer, Orde and Graham met a woman who stared at 'Sydney's dirty unsocked ankles', then lost her temper at his offer of 'three pence halfpenny' for the collection:

> 'Coppers! This is a silver collection!' 'That is all the money I have at all,' said Sydney. 'Oh get upstairs then,' shouted the woman – all this in front of the audience-people starting to come in ... We all went into the Audience Chamber, & Lindsay and some young man & Sydney & I were on a row of chairs facing the old women. They were terrible, dried old bones in mauve velvet hats ... The young man like a neat little snake read an introduction. When he came to us it was like this: 'Also we have – er – Mr Graham, who has, er, published one book of poems.' Long pause. 'And er – Miss Orde will read a poem.' Lindsay ... mentioned the poets of the Apocalyptic

school, included Sydney among the names ... Sydney, despite nervousness & obvious fed-upness, read well, as did I ... The only one that made the faintest feeling of stir was a short Soutar doric poem ... Sydney's own 'Many Without Elegy' fell entirely flat. The utter wash-outness of the whole affair was palpable to everyone, nor was it helped by the neat snake's bright winding-up of the proceedings, using words as: 'An extraordinarily interesting & exciting hour, with unique ...' etc. ... A thin old red faced white headed man at the back ... got up & spoke very loudly & long, beginning: 'You say MacDiarmid is the leading Scottish poet, well to my mind he's a very uneven writer, a lot of his stuff is just so much balderdash ... now why haven't you included any poems by Soutar?' – (We had – two.) ... As for these so-called poets of the New Apocalypse? ... Now G.K. Chesterton was an Apocalyptic poet, but these young men don't know about the rules of rhythm, they're just trying to draw attention to themselves ...' He was spluttery, & got the word 'Apocalypse' wrong each time ... I almost got the giggles, Sydney did once. He obviously did not realised, or remember, that Sydney had been introduced as such a poet. Some of the bones cottoned on, & the atmosphere was of embarrassment. The old man, I believe, was Herbert Palmer. The whole room from the beginning had been supremely aware of Sydney's no tie or socks or handkerchief, of his air of sweaty anarchy. He hated facing such an audience, & being stared at like an okapi or something. But Palmer's attack roused him, and he suddenly started an excellent, well-worded & very emphatic exposition of 'The rules of rhythm'. Lindsay, fearing the suddenly virile atmosphere, interrupted him & the meeting was over.

Since 1922, when he apologised to Yeats for oversharing 'the curdling vinegar of my mind', Herbert Palmer's disposition seems to have soured. With a Faber selected poems to his name (*Season and Festival*, 1943), he had recently been acclaimed in *Poetry Review* as 'A Major Luminary' and involved in the same pages in a controversy with Nicholas Moore, one of the principal Apocalyptic poets – or, according to Palmer, 'a jealous opportunist and unscrupulous modernist racketeer'. Palmer's blunders discredit his reactionary 'attack', but if only Lindsay had let Graham complete his 'emphatic exposition'!

Several windows open from Orde's flat, the point of intersection of the circles. Firstly, Graham 'is having a drink' at the Wheatsheaf, the Soho pub, in which, as recalled by Wright, 'the same crowd turned up night after night', including John Minton and Peggy Jean Epstein, daughter of the sculptor, both named in the letters. Amongst the crowd might have been poets such as Barker, Thomas, Gascoyne, William Empson and Patrick Kavanagh and painters such as Francis Bacon, Colquhoun, MacBryde, Gerald Wilde, Wilhelmina Barns-Graham and Lucian Freud. Reflecting on Auden's description of the thirties as 'a low dishonest decade', Robert Hewison summarises the dim view of the forties: 'the next ten years were to be worse'. Yet the title of his own study, *Under Siege*, is drawn from contrary reflections, by John Lehmann, editor of *Penguin New Writing*: 'I would rather have been in London under siege between 1940 and 1945 than anywhere else, except perhaps Troy in the time that Homer celebrated'.

Secondly, Orde and Graham have been invited to make up a panel, with Maurice Lindsay, editor of *Poetry Scotland* (and yet another contributor to *The Crown and the Sickle*), at an evening of Scottish poetry, on July 14th. This was one of a series of 'open meetings on Fridays at 33 Portman Square', headquarters of the Poetry Society, with a programme on offer in *Poetry Review* at the price of a 6d stamp. On the sole evidence of Orde's letter, this otherwise unrecorded event was a significant occasion in the rise of the Apocalyptic movement. Contrary to the received idea that this 'short-lived', if not 'ephemeral', movement had run its course by 1943, it had, at that date, yet to reach its height. In August 1943, the BBC Eastern Service broadcast a talk by Desmond Hawkins on *The Apocalyptic Poets*, for which, as the leading figure, Dylan Thomas had personally recorded 'A Saint About to Fall'. As the last in a series entitled *Modern English Verse*, produced by George Orwell and covering the twentieth century from *Georgian Poets* to *The Political Poets* of the thirties, it was a token of national recognition. A year on, the scene depicted by Orde is a paradigm of the simultaneous promotion and rejection of Apocalyptic poetry, which continued unabated throughout the forties.

Thirdly, three of the Scott Street irregulars, Graham, Creme and Archer, 'have been here today', 8 July, the first two sharing her flat. Fourthly, Orde's '5/- worth' with the 'bloody awful cover' (by art editor and founder of the Glasgow New Art Club, J.D. Fergusson) is *Scottish Art and Letters*, edited by Robert Crombie Saunders, who had been Archer's private secretary until 1942. Just out, the first number features five Apocalyptics, including art critic Robert Melville, whose review of the New Scottish Group, organised by Fergusson, points out their 'kinship' with Jankel Adler; and with Lindsay, organiser of the Poetry Society event, who contributes his finest poem, 'Earl Magnus Before Haakon on Egilsay'. His own first number, *Poetry Scotland: First Collection*, features seven Apocalyptic poets – or rather, 'including Sydney among the names', as in Lindsay's 'talk', make that eight. Graham appears in none of the Apocalyptic anthologies, but is as natural a choice to represent 'the Scottish writers of the New Apocalypse' assembled by Lindsay as is Thomas for the BBC. Orde's invitation to join the panel may have been suggested by

Graham, rather than by Lindsay, whom she had yet to meet, although, even in advance of publishing a single poem, she may already have been well-reputed in her own right as an honorary Scot. In the foreword to the 1945 exhibition of the New Scottish Group, Lindsay summarises the Venn diagram, connecting 'the work of these young artists ... with the feeling behind so much modern poetry': 'This vigorous reaffirmation of romantic values which has swept through all the European arts ... is a natural reaction against the crabbed classicism of the period between the two wars'.

'The Apocalyptic Feel of the Times'

The standpoint of Maurice Lindsay, Apocalyptic poet and editor and partisan promoter of neo-romanticism, contrasts with that of David Wright, the other figure, beside Graham, at the centre of the circles. Orde was in love with Graham, the deepest influence on her poetry and a shining exception, despite his dirty ankles, to the appalling behaviour, recorded in her letters, of other 'poetry blokes', including, sadly, Archer, on the verge of a nervous breakdown. On the (sole) evidence of the first of these letters, Wright, another shining exception, was in love with her:

> I have a feeling about you that it would be a loss not to tell you, that you have come comfortingly into my life as a strength. I know that this is neither a glamorous or perhaps even welcome kind of compliment, and I am not putting down now any other kind, purposely, but the point of writing that one is that you might not have guessed it. I have minded not having your country address, and the weekend feels more perilous because of that. Mostly I have found the rocks to be

boring and the charmers to be sandy, and it … is lovely to have a gentle and imaginative rock at half an hour's distance. You know I believe deeply in spontaneity, sincerity &, where possible, candour, & no tricks; so … it would be a needless loss not to tell you that I have that absolute certain happy feeling about you that you will never not be in my life, somewhere, and that it has been great gain to have met you. You will know me well enough now to read no more and no less than what I write in words. There is no invisible ink between my lines.

Graham never wavered in his admiration for Dylan Thomas ('I'd met my match'), but had little more inclination towards 'criticism' than Orde. Scattered across letters, reviews, memoirs and introductions to anthologies as it is, however, yet to be collected, and associated with the anti-intellectual Soho of legend and disrepute, Wright's criticism is of equal value to that of his chief antagonist, Donald Davie, the spokesman of the Movement. Complex as it is, both as regards Apocalyptic poetry and Julian's Orde's, it amounts to the best advocacy of mid-century visionary modernism on record.

Surprisingly, Wright had nothing but scorn for the Apocalyptic movement itself. The reasons for this in part account for his indifference to Orde's poetry during her lifetime and his own career as editor and anthologist, when he could have done much to bring her the attention he later sought on her behalf. In the 'personal memoir and appreciation' published in *PN Review* in 1978, he makes a heartfelt acknowledgement: 'Now I am able to value her, as I wish I had done while she was alive, as a poet'. Yet, at the same time, recalling 'the days when we used to show poems to one another when we met in some pub, or corresponded', Wright sticks to his guns: 'I think I had some excuse for not then being impressed as I am now by her poetry ... At any rate, the poems of Julian's that I knew were nearly all "forties" poems, many of them smudged by the surreal imagery of the period'. Wright condemns himself alongside Orde in his overview of a decade of poetry 'pocked with the endemic neo-romantic rhetoric to which our generation was exposed'. By the time his first collection, *Poems*, accepted by Tambimuttu in 1943, was finally published by Editions Poetry London in 1948, he was tempted to chuck his copy off the cliff to which his Cornwall cottage clung.

It is in his *PNR* 'Note' on Orde that Wright makes his most forensic diagnosis:

> The neo-romanticism of the 1940s infected nearly the whole generation that was born around the Great War in time for the next. Everybody had it, like measles; even those who are not now thought of as neo-romantics – Keith Douglas, Philip Larkin, Norman MacCaig for example – caught the infection to begin with. Few recovered; but I think that those who did, eventually wrote the better for that inoculation. The fever (for it was more of a malady than a fashion) was I think due to the impact of the sprung verse of Hopkins, ... and the almost coincident publication of *Finnegans Wake* and Yeats's last poems with the outbreak of a long-expected war; also to the near-mesmeric influence of two contemporary exploiters of language, George Barker and Dylan Thomas, whose poems caught the apocalyptic feel of the times and offered our generation a different fare to the politico-sociological gruel served by their immediate predecessors, the public-schoolboy left-wing Auden-Spender axis. (I hope it will be understood that I am not talking about the synthetic 'New Apocalypse', a 'movement' of the forties which was a conscious

attempt by reputation-makers at exploiting a spontaneous trend.)

A *Spectator* review of *The Faber Book of Twentieth Century Verse*, revised by Wright and John Heath-Stubbs in 1965, might explain his anxiety to avoid misunderstanding. 'Salvaging the Apocalypse' is one long sneer by Ian Hamilton, a contender for the title of Arch-Nemesis of the movement. His *coup de grâce* is a dismissal of 'these two champions of the Apocalypse'. Heath-Stubbs was mortified. Nevertheless, once a dogmatic mistake and a distinction on which Wright insisted have been clarified, the accolade might be shown to be justified after all.

To begin with, 'the synthetic "New Apocalypse"' was nothing of the kind. In the excitement of their response to Dylan Thomas, the poets who met to plan the first Apocalyptic anthology in the winter of 1938 anticipated the 'spontaneous trend' before 'the forties' had even begun. Denys Val Baker makes more accurate use of the same phrase in *Transformation* No. 3 in 1945:

> [A]s from about 1938, there has grown up the Apocalyptic group of writers led by J.F. Hendry and Henry Treece ... More recently the Apocalyptic movement has, or so it seems, merged into ... a loose and heterogeneous movement ... (indeed it is perhaps more of a spontaneous trend) but there is no doubt that its ideas are widely spread among contemporary little reviews.

Wright's scorn for the *movement* gives all the more weight to his startling endorsement of the *word* in an article on Watkins in *Nimbus*, in 1955, at the height of the later Movement. In order to rehabilitate the unfashionable poet, he sets out to redeem the far *more* unfashionable 'term':

[H]is affinities clearly lie with the poets that succeeded the Auden-Spender group ... To these writers, Barker, Thomas, Gascoyne, and Watkins, the term 'apocalyptic' seems naturally to belong; but unluckily this word was long ago hopelessly vulgarised and discredited by a movement invented by Henry Treece ... None of the poets I have mentioned appeared in [*The White Horseman*], with the exception of Watkins. But ... it is easier to conceive why his work should occur in a volume of 'apocalyptic' poetry than it is to understand what the other contributors were doing there. For Watkins' contributions strike one as poetry, and that poetry to be apocalyptic.

This is consistent with Abercrombie's dismissal of 'Mr Treece and the other horsemen of the Apocalypse' after pointed praise of Barker as 'apocalyptic', an example of the 'discrimination' which impressed Wright, from a perspective which influenced his own. Less interested in defining 'the term' than in poetry that lives up to it, Wright lets the simplest definition stand: '"of the nature of a revelation" ... seems to me to be as good a description of a poem as any'. Twenty years later, in 'Another Part of the Wood' (*Poetry Nation*, No. 4, 1975), a defence against Davie of 'the best work' of 'the forties', 'obscured, now as then', Wright again nominates a shortlist of genuinely 'apocalyptic' poets, making the number up to seven:

Three poets of stature ... emerged between 1940 and 1950 – Vernon Watkins, W.S. Graham, and Patrick Kavanagh. Keith Douglas might be added to this list ... [Yet] in 1950 ... Alan Ross in the *Listener* could discuss 'the poetry of the forties' without mentioning any of them, or even ... George Barker, David Gascoyne and Dylan Thomas.

Wright's classic anthology, *The Mid-Century: English Poetry 1940–1960*, is dedicated to David Archer, for his prescience in publishing four of the seven 'poets of stature'. Douglas apart, each of these seven is given more space than the four Movement poets put together. Reduced to two, contributors to the Apocalyptic anthologies fare even worse, yet as 'an imaginative response to the contemporary dilemma', *The Mid-Century* is itself, in Wright's own sense, 'apocalyptic'.

'Even the Central, Liquid Rock Moves in Me'

Orde's participation in Graham's happenings is conjectural, but two ms sonnets, amongst the earliest poems in her distinctively surrealist style, have Graham's prints all over them. Their rhyme words are in a column at the right, with a line constructed to end in each one, exactly as in Frame's account of Graham's technique at Sandyford Place: 'In preparation for the final draft of his poem, he liked to compile long lists of words ... typed out, one word below another'. Orde's lines do not quite reach the rhyme words that complete them, leaving a noticeable gap:

Treading the daisies down with steps of	silver
The ghost came swaying sideways to the	house
Followed by many who could never	rouse
Dogs from their sleep or butler with a	salver
Or wake a moth. These, like the shadowy	elver
Who slips away half round all seas, to	cows
In the clover by the country pond and	owes
Nothing but wonder – These followed the	miller

Into the house were sucked the flickering twelve
White shadows, till the house was a praying nation
Calling for cease of war when the extreme
Childhood of their fear begins to delve
Through the last webs of the grownup ration
And they cry to wake and know it's not a dream

The aleatory trick she may well have learned from Graham works. The way the ethereal ghost-story gives way to 'grownup' anguish is implicit in the transition from fairy-tale or nursery-rhyme words for the octet – 'silver', 'salver', 'cows', 'miller' – to those for the sestet in another key – 'nation', 'extreme', 'ration' – the last in particular immediately suggestive of the 'war'.

Her second published poem, in *Poetry Quarterly* in the summer of 1945, gives a deeper insight into the interrelations between her, Graham, Wright – 'all in the one number, you me and J' – and Thomas. The affinities between 'The Awaiting Adventure' by Orde and 'The Day and Night Craftsman' by Graham – not lost on the editor, who prints them on facing pages – are so strong that they could be spliced into a coherent composite poem (Graham's lines are in italics):

> The revolving lighthouse is adrift and lost –
> *Here's flame as dark as falling and ascension –*
> But oh! I am awake and running down
> The yellow slopes of my tomorrow's hopes!
>
> *Here where I hope and happen on a cindered hill*
> *Down the green guilds the children and the season*
> *Press shape in mud and chivvy language down.*
> The hierarchy of mountains does not speak,
>
> But the cool flowers, with a different life,
> *Jet through the meadows as they say the season*

Over and ever arriving, giving the rising
Seizure to summon the town, anyway fountain.

The jet of life has sprung its ecstasy:
I am in love with greater than I am,
And share the way of stone and star and lamb,
And even the central, liquid rock moves in me.

Here where the quick quays lie along the veins
There is about us more than a man's mind,
More than a ship's huge voyaging and end
Or the whole brass music of a gallant day.

Orde's fan-letter to *Poetry (London)* was also the most engaged
and perceptive criticism of Graham to date, preceded only by
a few friendly editorial remarks in *Life and Letters* by Robert
Herring and a well-disposed but tentative review in *Tribune*
by John Ormond. Each of her 'reasons' for finding him 'an
exciting writer' is illustrated by the *Poetry Quarterly* diptych:

(1) His poems differ from other young poets in that
they are all 'looking upward'; gladness, sympathy,
love, tolerance and a zeal for life characterise each
one; not a grumble, not a judgement among them. He
shouts for joy, yet there is no escapism. I find them
connected with life; when I read them they are of my
life and I see it as a richer and more glorious affair.

Echoed by Graham in a letter to William Montgomerie
in 1944 – 'They're young poems and win by an ascending
enthusiasm' – her emphasis is borne out by 'The Day and
Night Craftsman', which supplies a thesaurus entry for the
word 'upward' ('spires', 'ascension', 'reached', 'Jet', 'hope', 'rising',
'fountain', 'height'), copiously supplemented by 'The Awaiting
Adventure' ('sky', 'high', 'banners', 'wings', 'leaping', 'hopes',

'jet', 'ecstasy'). In view of the inwardness of her response, it seems clear that Graham's poems were indeed already part of her life.

Orde's second and third reasons comprise a nuanced account of Graham's indebtedness to Thomas, undisputed (least of all by the poet), but all too often and obtusely held against him:

> (2) Although his work is certainly 'Contemporary', yet he seems to have drawn the best from the whole range of English lyrical poetry rather from one modern group.

> (3) The seeming freedom of expression is actually confined within the most formal of rhythmic boundaries (a sort of primal integrity). Perhaps he comes closest to Dylan Thomas in his choice of language, though never in mood.

The 'one modern group' is the Apocalyptic movement, which would have done well to recruit Graham. The oversight is made good in *Poetry Scotland: Second Collection* by another migrant from the Scott Street Centre to Soho, Fred Urquhart, in a review of Lindsay's 1945 anthology, *Sailing Tomorrow's Seas*: 'Hendry, Graham and Scott belong to or are akin to the New Apocalyptic group'. By this date, Graham is resigned to the fate of *The Seven Journeys*: 'O the reviewers certainly go their mile. "It's a forgery of the poetic currency and of Dylan Thomas". But I suppose it's to be expected'. Both the affinity and the distinction suggested by Orde are clearly evident in Thomas's 'I Fellowed Sleep' (1933), notable for a similar set of synonyms, beginning with 'the upward sky' ('climbed', 'Reaching', 'stars', 'wings', 'tops', 'Raised', 'ladder'). A stanza snipped from Graham's poem (in italics) might easily be stitched into Thomas's:

Here where the quick quays lie along the veins
Arriving others, madmen to my tongue
Cry crimson through the warehouse and the squares,
How black the dark is in the innocent day,
How white the space under the sea's window.

Then all the matter of the living air
Raised up a voice, and, climbing on the words,
I spelt my vision with a hand and hair,
How light the sleeping on this soily star,
How deep the waking in the worlded clouds.

In all three poems, there is a tension between 'falling' and 'ascension', living and dying, in keeping with Hendry's definition, in *Kingdom Come* in 1943, of 'the apocalyptic element' as 'that particular vision which grasps elemental forces either in birth or dissolution'. Thomas's Freudian fable is darker than Graham's 'wholesome / Terrible meantime', itself more equivocal than Orde's ecstatic 'jet of life'. Yet it is Orde who comes closest to the blueprint of Hendry's specifications, 'The force that through the green fuse drives the flower', in her identification with the force that drives 'the central, liquid rock'. An account of Thomas's 'absolute poetry' by Linden Huddlestone, in *Penguin New Writing*, as late as 1948, applies equally to theirs: 'the spontaneous welling up of an intensely personal vision that is truly apocalyptic and which overloads the very words trying to convey it; and yet it irresistibly carries the reader on into unfamiliar regions'. As Orde reminds Wright, 'You know I believe deeply in spontaneity', a characteristic of the 'primal integrity' she values in Graham.

Finally, Orde anticipates Graham's most insightful critic, Tony Lopez, in identifying the image of the 'voyage' as central to his art, focussing on 'The Third Journey' from *The Seven Journeys*:

(4) I like the created grammar, poetry coming from the words and not the idea. In the *Third Journey* I think he tells us a lot about his feeling towards his makings of poetry. This voyage that he takes into the heart of poetry with himself as a 'Scholar of Seas'. 'My muse is a ship Exalted and rigged on the spray that your worlds present ...'

Lopez argues that Graham's suppression of *The Seven Journeys* created a mistaken impression that he published only 'short occasional lyrics' until the 'more extended works began with *The White Threshold*. On the contrary, as a 'source book' for the 'sequence of voyage poems', including 'The Nightfishing' and 'Malcolm Mooney's Land', *The Seven Journeys* 'contains in embryo almost all the subjects of his major works'. 'Graham's development ... was prefigured at the outset'; and in her appreciation both of his 'voyage ... into the heart of poetry' and the 'created grammar' by which it finds expression, Orde is on the right wavelength from the start.

'Our History is in Us and We in History'

The earliest example of her attunement is 'Highgate Afternoon', a declaration of love (which echoes a beautiful line in 'The First Journey': 'Stranding the stars on waking shoals of light'):

> I love. The musical houses are slanting into streets.
> My wide window draws in a population of cities ...
> O I have a planetarium of unsung stars for him!
> And my house is infinite and my window wide and
> my arms wide,
> Shoaled with the straying and creeping-in as they
> stretch for him ...

Because one parachuting seed, soft rocking on a
  breath
Might in Marazion grow a green city, lift Germoe
From its cobblestones or drum Pengersick Lane to
  Wheelhouse
To find his easy heart and bind with green his cara-
  van,
I will blow and I will blow my seeds to Marazion and
  Germoe ...

The long salt octaves are his sleep song there,
To roll his pillow in the home-sick miles of a sea's
  sigh.
How far that makes him seem ... how almost reach-
  ing goodbye ...
Wave upon wave upon wave of green seas slumber
  him brave.

A distillation of 'Highgate Afternoon', 'The Awaiting Adventure' also distils the ecstatic and ascending qualities Orde identifies in Graham as distinct from the 'mood' of Dylan Thomas:

The expert from the city tunes the trees
In far snowfields of sleep we may not cross.

The 'dear musician, all a world to westward' in Marazion, is the 'Dear stranger' who, in both poems, transmits 'wave upon wave' of music through the 'singing wires' of the 'city', like a telecommunications 'expert' installing overhead cable. (Deleted lines in the typescript of a slightly later poem, 'The Lonely Company', make this link explicit: 'They may write or paint for their living / Or mend telephones; their gift is one of loving'.) Although distilled *out* of 'The Awaiting Adventure', 'salt' is one of Orde's trademarks, occurring in over a dozen poems, including draft lines about 'The salty thigh of Cornwall', where she may have visited Graham. Its elemental, medicinal and erotic qualities outweigh any negative ones, comprising a symbol of the savour of life, or, as in the image of 'the salt gone out of the sea', of its desolating loss.

In June 1944, Orde thanks Wright for a poem entitled 'The Sea-Lost': 'I am so glad to be able to say honestly that I like it, & because I like it to be able to say what in it I would cut out, & most enjoy ... I read your poem to Sydney Graham who liked it very much'. Although objecting to 'azure wave' as 'a poetry cliché', she relents in consideration of its 'loveliest lines', 'I slung in tangle and the salt / submarine briar and the brine': 'Very lovely & sea-salty'. Unrepentant, Wright got it in the neck from Graham a year later, on exactly the same grounds:

> In this poem ... I find a kind of artificial classicism which I think comes from ... those coldly exotic words ... For me those words make the poem bloodless and artificial. The sea is not salt enough ... It is all too mezzanine, aquatile and aeolian for me.

In the same letter, however, he praises the poem which accompanied theirs: 'Your poem in *PQ* was lovely'. 'The Bay', one of the finest in Wright's rejected and never-yet-reprinted *Poems*, also shows the influence of Graham, again mediating that of Dylan Thomas (and Baudelaire):

> The dunes crumble here into the bay,
> a gurnard goes with his reflecting eye
> about his element, and four petrels
> cross their eight wings of love. The yellow dales
> possess their dwellers, a cottage, and sheep,
> a bird sings music to a certain shape.

Another climbs and stares above the bay.
I fasten thought on the spiralling feather
Till I drag down that plumage to the sea.
The tides are at my foot. The land I create,
Think the fortunate archipelago
Where the gull faltered, an El Dorado.

The reciprocity is startling. Wright, for his part, in a letter to a friend in 1965, turns conventional criticism on its head, not content with defending but actually preferring Graham's earlier style:

Sydney Graham was the first poet … whom I knew well. That would be 20 years ago; he taught me a lot. In those days he was very good … Then the needle stuck – was it in Finnegan, or Celtic alcoholism, or the vanity we all have; anyway he seems to have gone on writing the same poem, in almost the same words, since the early fifties.

This is the context of Julian Orde's poetry, as reflected in microcosm in her letters to Wright. The conclusion of 'The Awaiting Adventure' is her unassuming equivalent of the moment in *Little Gidding*, when, on a winter's afternoon early in 1941, 'History is now and England':

Stranger, met at last, this great beginning
Shall swing us through all times and all planes;
Though we but walk, are little, and have names,
Our history is in us and we in history.

The war impinges on Orde's poetry of the war years only, if at all, in this sense of 'history', as Graham, in *The Seven Journeys*, datelined like a Pathé newsreel, invokes it only as noises off:

History has run along my heart's boundaries
And webbed a creature, so making noisy war …
The eye is a lake. The sky is Neptune hovering.
May was my law. Nineteen fortytwo.

Wright recalls the composition, in Orde's Archway flat, of the poem Graham chose to read at the Poetry Society, quoted so warmly in her letter. Its title would imply a reference to the war:

> Many were the conversations that I had with Sydney
> at 49 Cholmeley Crescent … partly preserved because
> I had trouble in lipreading his heavy Scotch accent;
> I still have scraps of paper, and backs of envelopes,
> covered with his talk … about the technique of verse-
> making. He was at that time constructing (there is
> no other word for it) 'Many Without Elegy'. That
> poem … was meticulously planned; a blueprint … of
> the stanza-form, rhyme-scheme, metre, number and
> placing of syllables and beats to a line, set at the head
> of a sheet of paper before a word of the poem was
> written. Words, their weight, resonance, ambiguities,
> affinities and associations were his obsession.

In a context of family heritage and the 'scenery' of the Firth of Clyde, however, 'Many Without Elegy' is almost defiantly personal in its refusal to mourn the 'Many' at all, far less the 'few' of the Battle of Britain immortalised by Churchill. There is not a single image of WWII in Graham's wartime poetry; even such words as 'war' and 'warfare' ('my warfare wife locked round with making'), 'ruins' and 'rubble', for all their 'associations', make no direct allusion. In 'A Refusal to Mourn the Death, by Fire, of a Child in London' (published in May 1945), Thomas's objection to 'any further / Elegy' seems to echo Graham's prior refusal:

Here as the morning moves my eyes achieve
Further through elegy. There is the dolphin
Reined with searopes stitching a heart
To swim through blight. No I'll inherit
No keening in my mountainhead or sea
Nor fret for few who die before I do.

'Thomas appeared to value Graham's opinion', according to the Snows, and he, too, may have read the poem in advance of its publication in *2ND Poems* in August 1945, perhaps in the Soho pub where he showed Graham 'an early draft of "Fern Hill" … on the back of an envelope'.

Orde's only reference to the war, oblique as it is, occurs in 'The Lonely Company' (c. 1944), the 'bombs' reduced to a metaphor for the hostility of society to 'the bright figures of the just', yet nevertheless integral to the Apocalyptic scenario of 'the day of wrath' (Revelation 6:17).

No explanation blew a wider gate
Than finding how closely carried early and late
In what I must call the heart or breast
Are the bright figures of the just,
Those who, since the first splash of a stone,
Now, and tomorrow, are the best of us.

Born under Capricorn to be
Most criminal yet also the most free,
Who, after the mind takes them down
Into the bitter town,
Return with some weeping,
Gone soft with the gentleness of the homecoming;
The most afraid and best prepared for death
And the day of wrath.

They do not come with bombs
Yet are made unwelcome.
Above the sad-frocked and the flicker-eyed
They spike like stars.
I leave it to them, not nuns, to say my prayers,
And since this gate blew wide
Know we shall never be separated
For where they are there the heart goes along.
They are the company I would choose to die among.

The poem is an allegory of the comings and goings of the Soho crowd reported in the letters, identified in a draft as 'More than friends; poets or simply / Those, who by many reasons are much to be loved ... The most welcoming and least made welcome, the / Men of little means whose spirits are free'. Both the poem and the letter give an insight into 'Sydney's philosophy', in which, as in 'What is the Language Using Us For?', our deepest concern is for 'Each other alive', not as opposed to the dead, but as including them amongst 'the best of us':

It matters only in
So far as we want to be telling
Each other alive about each other
Alive. I want to be able to speak
And sing and make my soul occur
In front of the best and be respected
For that and even be understood
By the ones I like who are dead.

Concern for 'Each other alive' could hardly be more dramatically demonstrated than by Orde's readiness to grab her baby and dash to the aid of friends, matched by their concern, bleeding and distraught as they are, that such a scene was 'no place for babies'.

Undiminished by the return of Nessie Dunsmuir, her love for Graham is expressed in an untitled sonnet which shows an extraordinary empathy for his belief that the true artist must be 'maimed for the job' (several of his letters insist on the literal truth of this phrase from 'The Thermal Stair', carried over from a worksheet for an earlier sequence, 'The Dark Dialogues'):

> You were not here, you were never here
> Yet I wake with the barking dog in the dark
> With the sound of your ship grinding near
> The shipwrecking rock that your sombre heart
> Picks out for your bred-in-the-bone undoing,
> Your never-living-unless-you're-dying,
> To hurt yourself and stiffen and quicken your art.
>
> Because I love you and because I am
> As much yourself as any man or woman
> And because my manner of multiplicity
> Encourages me in thinking it my duty
> To dive to the bottom to know how the sea lives,
> – (Ever after carrying salt to the ocean) –
> I now have you to wake me as you cry for your loves.

It was Orde who introduced Graham to Messrs Foote, Cone and Belding, where he spent a few unhappy months as an advertising copywriter in 1950, but if their friendship faded in the fifties, the evergreen memory of 'the Julian Orde summer' illuminates Graham's poem for Wright:

> David the falling sun
> Stands on Highgate Hill
> Looking out for Julian
> Coming home from her job.
> In the Julian Orde Summer
> I remember the bicycles

Of lovers coming home
Laden with blue-bells
From the Highgate woods.

'The Simple Colourless Church Windows of Her Wings'

Two contrasting poems of the mid-forties illustrate the range
and subtlety of Orde's style, in which the keynote of 'ascending
enthusiasm' is occasionally varied by its dark obverse. 'The Upward
Rain' begins with a surreal, but benignly lyrical paradox: 'Green
climbs to the sky till the clouds are swelling with flowers'; in 'Eve',
on the other hand, there is a disquieting reversal: 'The garden
galloping / All its green / Down through my / Empty eyes'. In
context, there is nothing exuberant about the mordant enigma of
Eve's 'unkind / Birth', 'unkind' in its trauma, but also in its unique
estrangement from the gestation of human 'kind', formally
expressed by the spatial and syntactic dislocation of the rhyming
dimeters. The ordeal of the first breath, when an alien function is
activated by the intake of oxygen into the lungs, compounded by
the shock of a blinding glare of sunlight, the overwhelming inrush
of sensation, like a physical assault, and the ominous 'shadow / Of
Adam', combine to give Eve a nightmare awakening:

Sunblinded
        From my unkind
Birth, remembering
        The garden throwing
Itself on me,
        The windy
Lung's scream
        When the air jumped in,
The long shadow
        Of Adam, so:
Plurality.
        Quickest took me:

> The garden galloping
> > All its green
> Down through my
> > Empty eyes.

Two of Dylan Thomas's signature themes, prenatal experience and the pastoral bliss of 'Adam and maiden', are given a feminist twist in a way that has become commonplace, but that at this date was highly original. 'The garden galloping / All its green' echoes and subverts the Edenic final stanza of 'Altarwise by Owl-light', which culminates in phallic exaltation:

> Green as beginning, let the garden diving
> Soar, with its two bark towers, to that Day
> When the worm builds with the gold straws of venom
> My nest of mercies in the rude, red tree.

'All Gabriel and radiant shrubbery' for Thomas, Eden is imagined as the more traumatic for Eve because her prenatal experience is non-existent other than as a 'thin bone'.

> > I had started
> My double journey:
> > > Earth and history.
> Had never stepped
> > > Light as a child,
> Had never known
> > > Watery womb,
> Or turned over
> > > Inside a mother.
> A poor thing,
> > > My derivation,
> A thin bone
> > > Stood alone.

> Still am I seeking
> > Compensation.

A companion poem, entitled 'Eyes Alone', is as dark as Thomas's 'time-bomb', 'A Saint About to Fall'. Written in the shadow of Munich in September 1938, this poem is a mother's warning to her unborn child of a world of 'herods' on the march ('the eyes are already murdered, / The stocked heart is forced, and agony has another mouth to feed'). Orde replicates the unsettling personification of 'eyes', even more vividly in a draft of the poem: 'Without oneself, with but the power of seeing, / And in this Adam moment – what a view!' However, the masculine but implicitly universal perspective of Adam, or everyman, gives way to the lonely agony of Eve:

> As strange it is as Eve's defenceless waking
> When the garden surged into her naked eyes
> To meet no other summer green of memories.
> A rib stood staring, raped headlong by a garden.

'The Upward Rain' might seem almost too harmonious, if not for an unforgettable simile:

> Flashing wet metal, there is sudden arrival
> > of dragonflies,
> Held in the air by their rigid and quivering wings
> > like church windows.

Exactly the same simile appears in 'A Cranefly in September' by Ted Hughes, a tribute to Sylvia Plath in which his relentless sense of the inevitability of her death, but also of his own helplessness, finds allegorical expression in the creature 'exerting her last'. In a breath-taking allusion to Plath's final poem,

'Edge', the 'perfected vestment' is the 'toga' worn by the woman 'perfected' in death. Orde's windows are coloured, but Hughes adapts the image to the 'colourless' wings of the cranefly, with the same thin black lead 'camework' as stained glass:

> Her jointed bamboo fuselage, ... and her face
> Like a pinhead dragon, with its tender moustache,
> And the simple colourless church windows of her wings
> Will come to an end, in mid-search, quite soon.
> Everything about her, every perfected vestment,
> Is already superfluous.

In contrast to Hughes's gentle, wilting and bewildered cranefly, Orde's dragonflies seem to have flashed onto the scene from the 'furious arena' of 'To Paint a Water Lily'. Yet they must surely be reckoned amongst his numerous borrowings from the little magazines of the forties.

'Presented to Pain Down a Thousand Hairs'

When Wright sent a proposed selection of Orde's poems to three friends, C.H. Sisson, Geoffrey Hill and William Empson, all agreed 'that they are worth a volume', and all singled out 'Conjurors', which Empson 'particularly' liked, Sisson considered 'quite remarkable' and Hill double-ticked. Neither Sisson nor Hill was sure what to make of her, but Empson, who had been 'acquainted with her', but 'had never seen her poems before', was highly receptive to 'her note', appreciating her 'wonder at all experience', her 'beautiful ear' and 'unforced humour'. There was, however, a significant caveat: 'But it does not suit her to be surrealist, and the ones using that method ... confuse the overall picture; I should leave out ... "The Flying Child"'.

Here he is uncharacteristically wide of the mark. In fact, there is an intriguing interrelationship between 'Conjurors' and one of his proposed deletions. 'The Flying Child' combines the intensity of suggestion of pure surrealism with the 'singing line' which Empson missed in the poetry of the Movement, as it registers the hyperaesthesia of a child with a moth in her 'den of hands':

> A thief in despair, my hands were stones,
> And nothing so feeling as membrane moth
> (Presented to pain down a thousand hairs)
> Had ever cruelly crashed in the dark;
> And nothing so brittle and insect eye-lashed
> Had crackled and fluttered in such a den.
> (No voice it had, to print in the air
> A crippled copy of harm and hurt.
> That was the worst, the loneliest thought.)

The child's hands are at once as insensate as 'stones' and as sensitised as a nerve-end, the pain clinically intensified by the anodyne word 'Presented'. The trapped internal rhymes – 'despair' / 'hairs'; 'membrane' / 'pain'; 'crashed' / 'eye-lashed'; 'hurt' / 'worst' – amplify the crackle and the flutter – both of wings and of eye-lashes – of the voiceless but electrifying phenomenon.

In the final stanzas, hyperreality gives way to out-and-out surrealism, as a single 'moth' is subjected both to 'multiplication' and metamorphosis, first into a heraldic 'hind', then into 'birds', then into a 'cat', with a final rhyming line as emphatic as it is disorientating:

> A multiplication of pain – the moth.
> I saw the generations lying
> Between its wings. I peeled one off
> And watched it meet and change the sky
> With a hind's breast, with a life forgiven,

Black as a whistle, out of a deathbed.
And into birds they all were startled,
Till the ruffed and feathered air was shaken,
And with bird brows my head was circled.

Then the last moth fell, soft-bodied, foetal,
Flopped to the gravel; became a cat.
The garden ground crept forward with it,
It dragged the night behind its heel,
And wildest bird could not migrate from that.

A moth might well be 'startled' to find itself a bird, but it is the matter-of-fact tone of the line that is so poignant, as though we were reading a parable or fairy tale in which what is happening is both magical and straightforward. Yet, matter-of-fact as it is, the line would be killed stone-dead by a change of verb: 'And into birds they all were transformed'. The connotations of fresh beginnings, a sudden awakening (or, from a 'deathbed', resurrection) and wide-eyed surprise combine to uncanny effect. The title of the poem reinforces the sense of identification with the 'wildest bird', its inability to 'migrate' suggesting both its vulnerability to the strange night-cat and a longing for the mystical transmigration which cannot occur in this claustrophobic poem.

If 'The Flying Child' represents one extreme of Orde's style, 'Conjurors' might be the natural choice to represent the other. Cited in the 'Introduction', Wright's appreciation does justice to her 'masterpiece', in terms endorsed by Sisson: 'at first I thought this is going on too long in mere description, but the poem becomes not only reflective but dramatic as it proceeds':

Something has so altered in the night,
Surely the wind changed to make this?
The racking caterpillar gone

                    And a pale nymph lightly borne
Under the old thread. Might
            It be a ghost? The mask on its face
            Has a beak of gold. It is like a little fish!

It is like a waxen fish
            Filled with green leaves
                    With a veiny hint
                    Of two wings' imprint,
With a waist, with a twitch-
            Ing tail, with a sheaf
            Of yellow dots. It is hooded like a witch.

It has come among us hooded
            And it has no bones!
                    It cannot walk
                    It wears a long cloak
But is also naked;
            It is the skin round albumen,
            The caul, the bag about the yolk.

Moths are not butterflies, in fact the differences between the nocturnal moth and the butterfly of summer days explain the much commoner phobia of moths. Yet the poems are so closely related that the second might be described as a sequel to the first. The metamorphosis of insect into bird recurs as a hieratic image in the literal metamorphosis of the butterfly: 'It has a beak of gold'; but the closest parallel is between the two poems at their most introvertedly symbolic:

> Round the iron-clawed seats were deeper drifts,
> Arrowed with fish-bone, horned with twig,
> To screech a shoe on the glass and grit,
> On a button that opened a castle door.
>   'The Flying Child'

> Oh I cannot make it go
> Though I kill it with my eyes.
> It's a castle of glass
> It's a door I cannot pass.
> 'Conjurors'

'I fear the dark / With a double knock' sounds like a moment from the first poem, much more accurately described as 'a fancy, violent and old' than 'Conjurors' in which these words appear. Similarly, the powder of scales on a moth's wings, which, in 'The Flying Child', tarnish the 'hands' with a guilty 'Stain', like Lady Macbeth's 'damned spot' (prompting a literal echo of the play in 'dusty death'), might seem to be transfigured in the butterfly's 'dustings of ... beauty'. Yet in 'Conjurors', too, the context is one of 'guiltily' imagined 'cruelty' and harm. The collocation of 'castle', 'glass' and 'door' recalls Eliot's personal inventory of images with tentacular roots and the question which it prompts: 'Why, for all of us, out of all that we have heard, seen, felt, in a lifetime, do certain images recur, charged with emotion, rather than others?' There is, in fact, a naturalistic interpretation of the glass 'castle' in 'Conjurors' ('I put seven in a tray / With a window of glass'); nevertheless, towards the end of the poem we find ourselves, like St Paul, looking through dark glass, then encountering an unearthly apparition (1 Corinthians 13:12: 'For now we see through a glass, darkly; but then face to face'):

> As a face at window palely pressed
> Moves, leaving the glass dark,
> So now this bottle
> Darkens, though a full
> Rigged ship awaits tomorrow's test
> Of spindle spars and stays. The clock
> Tells fourteen days have passed in the ark.

Fourteen days, and then a crack!
   A skull-grey face with tendril-coiled
      Antennae; wet
      Wings, in folds yet
Of greenish gold with spots of black,
    And a grey fur back, walk like a child
    Unbalancedly into the world.

The ship in a bottle is a domestic image, like the 'spindle spars' of an Ercol chair such as may have furnished Spoode House or Durham Place, but, at the same time, on its allegorical voyage, it is in danger of shipwreck, as in maritime verse in which 'spars' are a synecdoche for disaster: 'They fired shots till the pirate's deck ... Was blood and spars and broken wreck'. In the same almost mock-heroic vein, 'the ark' has connotations both of Noah's ark, a refuge from the flood, and the ark of the covenant under 'the veil of the temple', which, at the moment when Jesus 'yielded up the ghost', was 'rent in twain' by an 'earthquake' (Matthew 27:50-54).

After the involutions of syntax and rhyme ('crack' / 'black' / 'back'; 'coiled' / 'folds' / 'gold') and a staccato series of monosyllables, the word 'Unbalancedly' enacts the ungainliness of the step-by-step progress in the awkwardness of the adverbial ending, but more subtly in the tilt between the capital 'U' and the downstroke of the 'y', a lopsidedness that the rhythm then so beautifully redeems, with the final uncoiling of the folded golden child 'into the world'.

The curious changes of pronoun as the caterpillar 'In *his* carpet coat' becomes the insistent '*It*', capitalised fifteen times at the beginning of a sentence or a line in five stanzas on the chrysalis, then, after its androgynous childhood, the imago takes flight on '*her* early wings', culminate in the truly 'mysterious' ending. There is, as Wright says in concluding his analysis, 'a strange triumph about the quiet closing lines, when, having broken the chrysalis, the imago emerges':

She walks like a boat on the beach
    Dragging her drying sails,
        While the last
        Memory of her past
Shakes from her tail: a bead
        Of amber dew, unnoticed as the shell
        That husked and housed her in its brittle walls.

Climber of curtains, long she'll not hang there;
    Taut are her wings and head-dress.
        She will feed on sweet
        Slippets but will never eat.
She will find her answering angel in the air.
        She will not lay her eggs upon nasturtiums' crease
        And will not remember the taste of the leaf.

Suddenly she is soundlessly flapping across the broad
    Floor of the air without a trial;
        The sun takes her
        Across to the blue buddleia.
Out of her depths in air she is not afraid.
        When she reaches the tree she finds it full
        Of her own shapes and becomes
                indistinguishable.

The wondrous appearance of the 'answering angel' crystallises the mysticism of the poem, in its fusion of alchemy, metempsychosis, fasting, prayer and the 'blind dive' into darkness after our 'flash of daylight' before ascent into the radiant pleroma. Butterflies 'feed' but 'never eat' because they only drink, or, subliminally, subsist on sweetness and light. Yet the Kabbalistic '*maggid*, or "Answering Angel"' is not divine, but, according to Harold Bloom, who cites a commentary on the *Zohar* by a sixteenth-century disciple of Isaac Luria, 'man-made': 'when a man leads a righteous and pious life … and prays with devotion, then angels and holy spirits are created from the sounds which he utters … and these angels are the mystery of *maggidim*'. The stanzas on the 'conjurors' in their 'Cells', 'Heads bent in a praying shape', might have been written of these 'saintly mystics of Safed', the Jewish community in Ottoman Galilee:

> Chosen as conjurors and given
> Cells that bloom like water flowers,
> They do not play
> But heartily try
> To prove with perfect conjuring
> Dear life, if dear enough, allows
> A blind dive into a hatful of shadows …

> For three days wait
> Heads bent in a praying shape,
> Contracted and stiffened until
> They recede from the surface dizzily, with pain,
> At speed they take leave of their eyes, legs, brain.

'Answering Angels give dream answers to waking questions', but also 'break into the waking dimension' and 'speak through the mouth of the prophet, independently of his will'. Unlikely to have read *The Book of the Answering Angel* by an anonymous kabbalist, dating from around 1500, Orde may have come across 'answering angels' in the writings of Martin Buber or the most notorious of occult 'conjurors', the Elizabethan polymath, John Dee. However, the mystical subtext, from the indignation at the 'meek / Giving-up of ghosts' (Matthew 27:50) in the opening description of the blackfly to the caterpillar which 'cast his shroud', has ultimately less to do with the Kabbala, or with Faustian conjuration and control, than with Keatsian negative capability and personalist ideas of emanation and immanent transcendence:

> Filled with the dying and the growing in the
> wrath
> Of their commission
> To achieve transfusion,
> Then I can break but not awake,
> Nor hurry that congealing drop of breath
> To build myself one butterfly on earth.

Then again, in 'Manichaean doctrine', '"Transfusion" is the term' for the 'transmutation of the light elements' of the soul, 'passing … through matter' before their 'release and restoration' (A.V. Williams Jackson). Reflecting on 'how treacherous time subdues us, how we are all subject to mutation', Giordano Bruno insists, in a gnostic discourse on 'our transfusion, or passage, or metempsychosis', that 'we must indeed await it with prayers'. To 'build' suggests a busy activity, like Noah knocking nails into the ark, yet this ethereal construction is no more to be hurried than autumn apples or evening dew, as in 'The Ship of Death' by D.H. Lawrence:

> Now it is autumn and the falling fruit
> and the long journey towards oblivion.
> The apples falling like great drops of dew
> to bruise themselves an exit from themselves …
> Have you built your ship of death, O have you?
> O build your ship of death, for you will need it.

The allegory of the poet's own ship of death – 'She walks like a boat on the beach / Dragging her drying sails' – is so unforced as hardly to occur to the reader. The phrase 'out of her depth' has a suggestion of peril if not panic, but the plural gives it a different feel, suggesting as much an ascent *de profundis* as the implicitly maritime 'depths' of the air itself. As the imago finds its kind and 'becomes indistinguishable', there is a similar sense of timeless unanimity with 'Each other alive' as in Graham's poetry, a fulfilment of his aspiration 'to speak / And sing and make my soul occur' in the visionary company of 'the best of us'.

'Step-Laddered to Where I Can't Be My Own Compasses'

It was one of Julian Orde's later poems which beguiled David Wright into a change of heart:

> Emily's parcel – a bundle of notebooks, a coloured scrapbook of poems written in familiar Italianate script, a couple of folders of typed copies – was not opened without some sinking of the heart. It's not easy to find the best words for 'this won't do'. Leafing through loose sheets in the typescript folders, a title at the head of one of them caught my eye – 'Death in Lyndale Avenue'. I picked it out, read it, and sat up. A seen thing, visually alive on the page; for me, a poem. But then I thought: I know Lyndale Avenue, I know Julian; the words seem vivid because the images relate to things I remember. Yet there was that opening stanza ...

> Step-laddered to where I can't
> Be my own compasses, I
> Measure the years ahead by
> The white windows I'll paint.

Beginning with a metaphysical conceit inspired by Donne, this poem is nevertheless, as Wright observes, a 'statement' of 'exact precision', 'moving because made from a standpoint both detached and involved'. As theorist of the Movement, Donald Davie would have approved, as also of 'Two Elements', closer to the Empsonian ideal of the fifties than most of *New Lines*.

However, another poem from the same late group of five, 'Mendel's Garden', is altogether more elliptical, a vertiginous image subverting the closure of rhyming tetrameters:

> So we go on, the iron papers,
> Appropriating starry fields
> To reckon under roof, keepers
> Of the old, statistical yields,
>
> Late workers in planetary light,
> Compounded of the same blue clay
> In which we love and fight
> And dream blue nights away,
>
> Eugenists of efflorescence
> Culturing our nightmare city
> With iron gnashings, brokerage, pence,
> Wanting a monk's serenity.
>
> Old scientists, so we go on,
> Stumbling upon nothingness
> Late in life, all floor gone
> On which to kneel and make redress.

Quirky, quicksilvery, all about wings, but with sudden, unfathomable depths, Julian Orde's poetry is itself 'elemented differently', with substantial traces of 'nothingness', 'nightmare' and vertigo in the compound, but finding its quintessential expression in the plenitude of 'Conjurors'. This magnificent poem saw the light in *Poetry Nation* in 1976; and again in the beautiful Greville Press edition of 1988, with an introduction by Wright. The selection printed in *PN Review* in 1978 is an excellent showcase. Fifty years after her death, it is high time for her first collection.